THE JAPANESE SOCIALIST PARTY
AND NEUTRALISM

D1607690

The Japanese Socialist Party and Neutralism

A STUDY OF A POLITICAL PARTY
AND ITS FOREIGN POLICY

J. A. A. STOCKWIN

Senior Lecturer in Political Science
The Australian National University

MELBOURNE UNIVERSITY PRESS

LONDON AND NEW YORK: CAMBRIDGE UNIVERSITY PRESS

First published 1968
Printed in Australia by
Melbourne University Press, Carlton, Victoria 3053
Registered in Australia for transmission
by post as a book

COPYRIGHT; NO PART OF THIS BOOK MAY BE
REPRODUCED IN ANY FORM WITHOUT PERMISSION

SBN 522 83838 3
Dewey Decimal Classification Number 329.952
Aus 67–2211

Text set in 11 point Georgian type

To Katrina

who, at six weeks,
accompanied her parents
to Tokyo

81391

PREFACE

The Japan Socialist Party is one of the few social-democratic parties of any significance in the non-western world. As the major opposition party in Japan it has conspicuously failed to follow the patterns set by social-democratic and labour parties in Western Europe and Australasia. It has failed either to shed its Marxist heritage or to appeal to broad sections of the electorate with pragmatic and flexible policies. At the same time its organization and many aspects of its political behaviour are very much those of a 'traditional' Japanese political party: the personal faction, acting almost as a pseudo-family, is the dominant intra-party group. Personalities count for at least as much as, and probably more than, policies or ideologies.

It is in this paradoxical political context that the party formulates its foreign policy, the dominant though not unchallenged theme of which has been neutralism. In a sense neutralism has been a barometer of factional struggle within the party. It has been most easily accepted when left wing and right wing factions are well balanced, and has become distorted, or has even been tacitly repudiated, when the balance is less equal. The party, and thus its neutralist policies, have repeatedly been subject to stronger pulls from the left than from the right, so that the balance represented by neutralism has been frequently upset in practice. Recent events such as the Sino-Soviet dispute and the war in Vietnam have considerably added to the party's problems by making it harder for it not to come down conclusively on one side or the other. At the same time the perennial root causes of these problems lie more in the realm of organization and political behaviour than of external variables.

It would be misleading, however, to suggest that the foreign

vii

policies of the Japanese socialists are not worth discussing for their own sake, as an integral part of the lively national debate on Japan's international orientation which has been an important feature of her political scene since World War II. In arguing for a Japanese foreign policy independent of the United States the socialists have had behind them a substantial segment of educated Japanese opinion, not confined to the ranks of committed left wing activists. The rationale of such a view requires careful scrutiny.

In the course of the study I have tried to keep both these aspects in view.

This book is based on a doctoral thesis entitled 'The Neutralist Policy of The Japan Socialist Party' which I completed at the Australian National University in 1964. It has now been substantially revised and brought up to date. The work is based almost entirely upon Japanese-language sources and on interviews with participants; all the translations from the Japanese are my own. Between 1960 and 1964 I was a Research Scholar in the Department of International Relations of the Research School of Pacific Studies of the Australian National University. Of this period I spent fifteen months in 1962–3 in Tokyo, where I was attached to the Institute of Social Science (*Shakai Kagaku Kenkyūjo*) at Tokyo University. Subsequently as a Lecturer in the Department of Political Science of the School of General Studies of the Australian National University I paid a second visit to Tokyo from December 1964 to February 1965.

In Australia my principal thanks go to my thesis supervisor, D. C. S. Sissons, for his perceptive advice and criticisms. I also wish to express gratitude to Professors J. D. B. Miller and A. L. Burns, who at various times shared the burden of supervision, and to D. Hindley (now at Brandeis University). I am grateful also to Professor W. Macmahon Ball of the University of Melbourne, who was an examiner of the thesis and has given me some valuable suggestions for its revision. Professors L. F. Crisp and B. D. Beddie have both greatly encouraged me in the later stages of this project. I also owe a great deal to A. Watanabe and H. Fukui, who while Research Scholars at the Australian National University have allowed me to profit from their deep knowledge and study of the dynamics and personalities of

Japanese politics. For the same reasons I am grateful to S. Katō, who recently spent a year in Canberra as Visiting Fellow at the university. I must also thank the Australian National University for financing my first field trip to Japan and for giving me financial assistance for my second trip. I am grateful to Mrs W. Kieweg, who undertook the typing of the final manuscript. In North America I am indebted to Professor Robert A. Scalapino, of the University of California at Berkeley, who was an examiner of the thesis and has since made useful suggestions. I have also greatly profited from many discussions (in Tokyo face to face and later by correspondence) with Donald C. Hellmann, presently of Swarthmore College. The same is true of Frank Langdon of the University of British Columbia.

Those in Japan to whom I am indebted for advice, encouragement and information are too numerous to mention but I should single out Professor S. Hayashi of the Institute of Social Science of Tokyo University who acted as my supervisor in 1962–3, to Professor K. Takahashi, Director of the same Institute at the same period and Professor T. Ariizumi, who had become Director when I returned the second time. I must also thank Professor T. Ishida, of the same Institute, and Professor J. Masumi of Tokyo Metropolitan University for many useful discussions both in Tokyo and in the course of a visit they both paid to Canberra in 1964, when they addressed a seminar on modern Japan in the Research School of Pacific Studies of the Australian National University.

While in Tokyo I spent a considerable part of my time at the National Diet Library, whose Newspaper Cutting Section was particularly useful. I am very grateful to D. Nakai of that section for his assistance in locating material, and to S. Misawa, formerly of the Library's Legislative and Research Division (now a professor of Political Science at Saitama University) for the extraordinarily unselfish way in which he gave up his time to answering my questions.

Many members of the Japan Socialist Party and associated organizations were kind enough to give me their time for personal interviews and to supply me with information. I want also to thank all those JSP Diet Members who responded to my questionnaire, the results of which are set out in the appendix.

I am particularly indebted to the following four individuals connected with the party for the exceptionally great interest they showed in my research: S. Fujimaki, T. Kawakami, M. Uezumi and F. Yamaguchi (now of Tōkai University).

Finally, I wish to thank my wife Audrey, to whom this book owes much.

CONTENTS

CONVENTIONS

The following conventions have been observed:

1 Japanese names are written in the original order, that is, with the surname first and the personal name second.

2 The Japanese language normally does not distinguish between 'neutrality' and 'neutralism'. Therefore in quotations I have used one or other according to the context. The exception, however, is the term 'positive neutrality' (*sekkyoku chūritsu*). Here, since the term as a whole represents an attempt to translate 'neutralism', it would have been redundant to talk of 'positive neutralism'.

3 The English-language title of *Nihon Shakaitō* has been given as 'Japan Socialist Party' (JSP). This is now the official English name of the party, although the mistranslation 'Social-Democratic Party of Japan' (SDPJ) was its official name between 1945 and 1962.

4 In citing major daily newspapers in footnotes I have omitted the word *Shimbun* (newspaper). This applies to the *Asahi, Jiji* (now defunct), *Mainichi, Tōkyō, Yomiuri*. In lesser known newspapers (including party publications) the word has been retained where applicable. All newspaper references are to morning editions, unless otherwise indicated.

GLOSSARY

Chūkanha	Centre faction
Heiwa Dōshikai	Association of Friends of Peace
Heiwa Mondai Danwakai	Discussion Circle on Problems of Peace
Gensuikyō (Gensuibaku Kinshi Nihon Kyōgikai)	Japan Council against Atomic and Hydrogen Weapons
Kōza-ha	'Kōza' faction
Nihon Shakaitō	Japan Socialist Party
Rōnō-ha	'Rōnō' faction
Shakai Taishūtō	Social Masses Party
Shakaishugi Kyōkai	Socialist Association
Shinjinkai	New Man Society
Shinsambetsu (Zenkoku Sangyōbetsu Rōdō Kumiai Rengō)	National Federation of Industrial Trade Unions (New *Sambetsu*)
Sōdōmei (Nihon Rōdō Kumiai Sōdōmei)	Japanese Federation of Trade Unions
Sōhyō (Nihon Rōdō Kumiai Sōhyōgikai)	General Council of Trade Unions of Japan

xiii

ABBREVIATIONS

ASC	Asian Socialist Conference
COMISCO	Committee for the International Socialist Conference
DSP	Democratic Socialist Party
ICFTU	International Confederation of Free Trade Unions
JCP	Japan Communist Party
JSP	Japan Socialist Party
LDP	Liberal–Democratic Party
LSP	Left Socialist Party
NATO	North Atlantic Treaty Organization
PCI	Partito Comunista Italiano
PSI	Partito Socialista Italiano
RSP	Right Socialist Party
SCAP	Supreme Commander, Allied Powers—a term used to indicate the Occupation authorities in general
UN	United Nations Organization
WFTU	World Federation of Trade Unions

1

NEUTRALISM: THE WORLD SETTING AND JAPAN

Japan, governed since 1955 by a single conservative party enjoying a comfortable majority of seats in both Houses of the National Diet (Parliament), has long been regarded as a rare example of stable government and of moderate, essentially pro-American foreign policies. The main opposition party, the Japan Socialist Party (JSP), in contrast, whose only spell in office was as part of a coalition government in 1947–8, has most frequently been dismissed as a party in permanent opposition.

The most recent Lower House elections (January 1967) suggest that the JSP under its present leadership has failed to pull the party out of this rut. The party's morale, however, recovered in April 1967 with the election for the first time of a candidate backed jointly by the Socialists and Communists to the vital governorship of Tokyo. In the January general election the ruling Liberal-Democratic Party (LDP) also lost seats and for the first time failed to win 50 per cent of the votes cast. The beneficiaries were minor parties.[1] It still seems not impossible that the LDP could lose its absolute majority of Lower House seats in the early 1970s, especially if there were to be defections from its own ranks. (The party's internal cohesion has always been somewhat precarious.) In these circumstances it might possibly be succeeded by a centre-left coalition in which the JSP would necessarily be the leading element. At present the chances of such a government being particularly viable do not look great, but then the same could have been said of the warring conservative factions before they amalgamated in 1955. The slow but steady electoral trend of recent years away from the LDP is in the main a result of the long-term demographic

and social changes accompanying post-war economic growth.[2]
At the same time Japanese electoral behaviour in recent years
has been such that party fortunes seldom fluctuate much from
one election to the next. (The reasons for this are discussed in
chapter 12.)

For most of the period since 1950 JSP foreign policy has been
premised on some variant of 'neutralism' or 'non-alignment',
and has been categorically opposed to Japan's existing security
arrangements with the United States. Moreover, the party has
gone further than most neutralists in other countries by advocating *unarmed* neutralism as a serious policy. Many western
writers examining the party and its foreign policies have been
impatient or even hostile towards views that seem to them at
best impracticable and at worst disingenuous. One writer, for
instance, divided neutralists in the party into 'pseudo-neutral-
ists' (whom he evidently regarded as crypto-communists) and
'sentimental neutralists' (seen as unwitting communist stooges).[3]

This book, while in no sense an apologia for the JSP nor for
a neutralist Japan, represents an attempt to understand as dis-
passionately as possible what Japanese socialists mean when they
talk of neutralism, and what kind of party it is that puts forward this particular set of policies. It should become evident
from the analysis contained in this book that the JSP, despite
its adherence to an extremely doctrinaire mode of expression,
is a far looser and more openly structured party than the Japan
Communist Party (JCP). Its main weaknesses, indeed, stem
more from the traditional Japanese character of its decision-
making processes than from its predilection for quasi-Marxist
reasoning. The JSP has much in common with the LDP, both
in the particularistic motivations of their respective politicians
and in the trend which has led both parties to become the
creatures of outside interest groups. (The LDP is at least as
weak in the face of pressure from government ministries and
big business groups as the JSP is dependent on trade unions.)
Contrary to widely accepted belief, a great deal of pragmatic
bargaining is carried out on all but the most contentious issues
between the government party and the socialist opposition. This
is likely to become greater, not smaller, if electoral support for
the LDP continues to decline.

Unlike the situation in countries where a bipartisan foreign policy has been accepted practice, in Japan the issues of Far Eastern international relations have been fought out between government and opposition with a singular hostility and divergence of purpose. Few domestic issues have aroused such bitterness. Yet even on foreign policy the two sides are not entirely without means of communication and understanding. To a considerable extent the views of the left wing of the LDP overlap with those of the right wing of the JSP, especially when it comes to discussing the China question. The socialists, moreover, have a number of excellent issues with which to attack the government at points where it feels itself to be vulnerable to criticism. When they accuse the government of passivity in foreign affairs, of subordinating Japanese interests to those of the United States, or of forfeiting the opportunity to increase trade with Peking, they are touching on a sore spot: the government is well aware, in the presence of revived nationalist (though not ultra-nationalist) feeling in Japan, of the little room for manoeuvre which it has so long as it maintains its present international alignments.

What then is the rationale and what are the antecedents of the alternative foreign policy which the socialists propose? In order to answer this question satisfactorily the first and most obvious point to be made is that neither policies nor the circumstances in which they are formulated stand still; nor do the personnel who devise them remain unchanged. 1950, when Japan was still under American Occupation and not yet recovered from the physical and psychological blows of 1945, was a far cry indeed from 1967, with Japan the most powerful and prosperous nation in Asia and flexing her muscles for a significant role in world politics. The international context has changed at least as much over the same period. The bipolar world of the cold war, in response to which neutralism first made its appearance in India, has given way to a much more complex international polycentrism. The principal threat to world peace is now thought to come less from the possibility of nuclear war between the two 'super-powers' than from the consequences of possible nuclear proliferation among a dozen or so countries of the second rank. The flashpoint has moved from Europe to

Asia, and within Asia the conventional battle-lines of Korea have ironically given way to the scattered but equally deadly guerrilla fighting of Vietnam. Meanwhile, as the Japanese themselves are fond of saying, the east-west problem is becoming less important than the 'north-south' problem—than the increasing discrepancy of standards of living between the advanced and developing countries.

All this is well known; what is perhaps less widely understood is the nature and origin of neutralism as an approach to world politics, and its relation to traditional neutrality. Before turning specifically to Japan and to the JSP, we must briefly examine the terminology and ideas involved.

The word 'neutral' is characteristically ambiguous. It can denote either a state of mind or a pattern of behaviour (or both at the same time). If 'I am neutral' only describes my state of mind, it means that as between two or more alternatives, I have no personal preference. If it describes my behaviour, it means that I do not actively take sides. This leaves open three possibilities: I may have no personal preference and not take sides; or I may have a personal preference but nevertheless not take sides; or I may (though this is much less likely) take sides without having a personal preference. Similarly, a neutral nation-state may not only stay out of wars and alliances, but also make no distinction—tacit or open—between its neighbours; or it may keep out of wars and alliances despite the fact that one neighbour or set of neighbours is preferred to another. (The third possibility can be safely disregarded.)

Now, in a world divided along purely power-political lines and characterized by local wars between individual small states rather than large-scale confrontations between modern super-powers and their respective allies, the chances not only of remaining aloof from conflicts but also of staying genuinely impartial may be quite considerable. The presence, however, of exclusive and incompatible ideologies may make this much more difficult. If a country manages to remain neutral in these circumstances, its subjective impartiality may well be seriously in doubt. Switzerland or Sweden, for instance, would hardly be impartial between capitalism and communism though they would presumably strive to remain neutral, if that were possible or meaningful, in a war between the Soviet Union and the United States. Their neutrality, in other words, would be essentially a matter of behaviour. In this regard there is little difference between neutrals and neutralists, since both in the modern world may find genuine impartiality very hard to maintain. Nevertheless, both have on many occasions been subjected to bitter criticism from widely different quarters on the ground that the refusal of commitment means immoral or unenlightened indifference. This criticism is mostly based on a neglect of the distinction made above. Neutrality and neutralism have in recent times mostly been founded in conscious acts of policy designed to achieve specific ends. Whether those ends relate purely to the interests of the country in question or to wider considerations is another problem to which we must now turn.

Neutralists have generally held that their policies are fundamentally different from those associated with 'traditional' neutrality. Indeed the preference often shown for the term 'non-alignment' rather than 'neutralism' results from a desire to avoid being associated with the concepts of neutrality prevalent before World War II. The main alleged difference between neutralism (or non-alignment) and neutrality is that neutralism is 'positive' while neutrality is merely 'negative'. In other words, whereas the neutral nation merely seeks to avoid its own involvement in war, the neutralist nation seeks (probably in concert with other like-minded powers) to make a positive contribution to world peace.

This distinction, however, needs to be subjected to close scrutiny. The idea that neutrality in its classic European context was a 'negative' concept—that it had no constructive purpose in international relations, that its effects could even be harmful and that it was at best an instrument of national selfishness—was the result of an analysis of neutrality made during the period of the League of Nations.[4] Neutrality, however, evolved through several centuries of European history, and it did not always have the same connotations. The period during which neutrality gradually developed its 'modern' characteristics was the classic period of the European balance of power, from the Treaty of Westphalia to World War I. This was a period characterized by local wars, in which neutrals could hope for relative security. Morgenthau has pointed out that the evolving concept of neutrality still included the idea of war as a legal instrument of policy, and therefore it was assumed that any nation had the right to intervene on one side or the other as it saw fit.[5]

During the nineteenth century a whole series of obligations came to be placed upon the neutral—obligations of a stringency much in contrast with the easier neutrality of the eighteenth century and earlier—such as not to assist belligerents with manpower or arms, not to allow forces of belligerent nations to use neutral territory for their operations, and so on.[6] Under the League of Nations, however, neutrality came to be regarded with strong disfavour. This was because one of the League's most fundamental principles was a distinction between lawful and unlawful war, and also because all its members were obliged to assist a nation waging lawful war against unlawful aggression.[7] The widespread unpopularity of neutrality between the wars was because it was considered incompatible with such duties.

Even between the wars, however, opinions were not lacking from representatives of the neutral nations themselves, challenging this judgment. One writer, in 1939, attacked current definitions of neutrality which spoke of it in a negative fashion as 'impartiality' and 'non-participation', and proposed instead that it should be defined—more in keeping with the historical aspirations of neutrality—in terms of the very positive aim of keeping nations out of war, 'with all the moral and economic decay that accompanies it'.[8] Similarly, the negative attitude of the League towards neutrality was rejected by the United States, which pursued a policy of isolationism rationalized in much the same way.

Neutralism originated in the foreign policy of Nehru and other non-western statesmen during the late 1940s and early 1950s. They maintained that by refusing to take sides in major international confrontations, and especially by refusing to join cold war alliances, they should be able to work effectively for world peace.[9]

The altruistic, 'positive' content in neutralism is undeniable. During the 1950s India and other countries following her example acted as mediators in international disputes in a way which would scarcely have been possible had they been 'aligned'. Their influence on the policies of the United Nations was also very striking and frequently constructive. It is not, however, possible to sustain an absolute distinction between neutrality and neutralism in this regard. Neutrality, as we have seen, was perhaps not entirely self-regarding. Neutralism, on the other hand, was not completely free from what were often called 'negative' characteristics. In the speeches of Nehru and of other neutralist leaders the element of national interest was rarely absent. To say this, of course, is in no way to refute neutralism or to brand it as insincere. For the most part it represented genuine concern both for world peace and for national interest— a by no means incompatible combination. As a political phenomenon, however, it obviously has to be studied in terms of underlying motivations.

Neutralism as a policy of governments has generally been confined to ex-colonial countries of the underdeveloped world (though there are exceptions) and has proved particularly attractive to national liberation movements transformed into ruling élites. One writer goes so far as to say that 'the whole of neutralist doctrine could be described as a quest for distinctive, intellectual expression of independence, and starts from the assumptions of a given independent statehood.'[10] The leaders of such countries, unless they happen to be communists, have not wished to come under undue Soviet or Chinese influence, but they have wished even more strongly to assert their independence from the west. Where, as often, these leaders have been more or less socialist in outlook, their rejection of military or other ties with the west has been influenced by an implicitly or explicitly Leninist interpretation of western (especially American) 'imperialism' and 'exploitation'. Other, more pragmatic considerations have also played their part. There are countries whose internal problems are so great that alignment with either the Soviet or American bloc might seriously threaten domestic cohesion. Policies of non-alignment have been seen as a means of avoiding military entanglements and excessive expenditure on armed forces. (In any case such expenditure is quite beyond the resources of many countries in question.) They have also been regarded as a method of avoiding irksome restrictions on trade, and have made it possible for certain favourably placed nations (the United Arab Republic is a good example) with skilful manipulation of both sides to maximize the flow of foreign aid.[11]

From a strategic point of view, neutralism was a product of the world situation of the cold war period. This gave to neutralism a very different rationale from that of pre-World War II neutrality. The conditions which served to protect certain neutral nations against involvement in war were obsolescent in the early 1940s and had apparently ceased to apply altogether by the 1950s. Countries like Switzerland sought to ensure that in a war the gains that would accrue to a belligerent committing aggression against them would not more than outweigh resultant disadvantages for the belligerent. This entailed military preparedness up to a level greater than that normally contemplated by a nation of comparable size. In some cases special geographical features facilitated the task of defence.[12]

With the invention of nuclear weapons the possibility of a neutral deterring by conventional means an attack from a nuclear power, if that power were credibly prepared to use its nuclear capacity, virtually disappeared. (The qualification, however, is important.) In a nuclear war the only guarantee of security for a neutral relying on conventional weapons would be geographical remoteness from the scene of conflict, but the global nature of modern strategy makes this scarcely applicable. The likelihood of a neutral escaping conquest or destruction in a large-scale nuclear war was thus reduced to a question of chance and had little to do with neutrality or non-neutrality.

The rise of neutralism after World War II was therefore premised on quite other strategic considerations than those of traditional neutrality. For one thing, nuclear weapons now provided their own rationale. Certainly in the 1950s the forces which a small nation could hope to deploy had never before been so inferior to those of the Soviet Union and the United States. While this seemed to remove the old reasons for neutrality, it also provided a powerful argument for opting out of the 'balance of terror' which nuclear weapons had produced. Since there was little sense for a non-industrial power in trying to compete with the super-powers in manufacturing its own nuclear weapons, and since a military commitment to the American alliance could impose unwelcome, expensive and possibly dangerous obligations, it was natural enough that a number of these countries should seek a third road for their security and prosperity.

Moreover, neutralism was first propounded at a time when almost every issue of world politics was subordinated to the cold war. This had a profound effect on the nature of local war, since every border dispute and every revolution, especially in more sensitive areas of the world, became enmeshed in considerations of global strategy. By rival security pacts and multilateral military alliances, each side sought to prevent the other from expanding its sphere of influence. Neutralism sprang from the all-embracing character of this rivalry, with its total ideological commitments. It challenged the claim, expressed on both sides, that 'he who is not for me is against me'. In its more extreme form it was expressed as a 'third force', or 'third bloc', as put forward by the Praja Socialist Party of India. This was a 'plague on both your houses' view of both east and west, with racial as well as Marxist overtones, as seen in the phrase 'white imperialism'.[13] Nehru repudiated the doctrine in this form, denying that developing countries, with their diverse interests, could or should form a bloc. The anti-colonialism, however, of many neutralist statesmen predisposed them against commitment to the American alliance.

Thus the essential differences between traditional neutrality and post-war neutralism could be expressed in the following terms: The aim of the neutral was to escape involvement in war. Its method was to deter aggression, in the last resort by its own unaided effort. It succeeded when belligerents agreed to respect its neutrality, or if it possessed a credible deterrent. The aim of the neutralist was to escape involvement in rival power blocs and to diminish the likelihood of world war between those blocs. It could not, however, seriously expect to escape the effects of a world war should one break out. It did not place much stress on the development of its own deterrent capacity, except for the needs of the local power situation. The method which it sought to apply, however, was that of reducing the dangers inherent in an eyeball-to-eyeball confrontation between the two blocs, both by acting as a kind of buffer, and by exerting pressure for peaceful solutions to disputes in the UN and elsewhere.

The neutralism that has been referred to hitherto was a type of foreign policy that developed in the particular conditions of the decade from 1950 to 1960. From about 1960, however, these conditions began to change in significant respects and neutralism itself came to be stated in somewhat different terms. First of all, what have been termed 'polycentric' tendencies were gradually making their appearance in both the communist and western power blocs. The rifts between the People's Republic of China and the Soviet Union, and to a lesser extent between France and the United States, are only the best-known examples of this. This meant that local wars were once more not necessarily to be thought of as the flashpoints of a global conflict. Take, for instance, the Sino-Indian border dispute of 1962. It was a limited war fought on conventional lines between two countries, neither of which at the time possessed nuclear weapons, and without the intervention or even the whole-hearted support of the two original super-powers. The fact that India was a belligerent in a war of this nature did not necessarily affect the logic of her neutralism, since it could be rationalized as a 'local war'. On the other hand the potential scale of the dispute, the apparently formidable nature of China, and the fact that India proved inadequately able to defend herself without outside help, indicated that the original premises of her neutralism no longer fully applied. Not only had she become a party in a major conflict and thus had to fall back on military aid from the super-powers, but the bipolarity of international alignments—in which Nehru had seen the greatest threat to world peace and thus a major justification for neutralism—was slowly breaking down.

Did this mean that neutralism was obsolescent because its main objective was now being realized? In a sense, yes: neutralism as formulated by Nehru had been very much a phenomenon of, and a response to, the cold war. After 1962 the international standing of Nehru's doctrines tended to diminish, partly because of the difficulties of India herself and partly because of the radical transformation of the overall world situation. This did not, however, mean the demise of neutralist ideas.

Indeed, what is generally called 'non-alignment' is the accepted stance in foreign policy for a majority of 'developing' countries. This is now a rather vague term which may cover a variety of types of mutual arrangement with western and communist bloc powers. It still implies, however, a determination to remain outside any open military alliances with major powers, and to remain free to deal with any or all of them. Meanwhile a sense of common interest in world peace and of general community of interest against the advanced industrial powers has not entirely departed from among the developing countries, and finds expression in the UN.

A further most important innovation in the world scene of the 1960s was the doctrine of the 'independent deterrent'. This was based on a newly realized fact of nuclear strategy, that even a nuclear force that is many times outnumbered by the nuclear capacity of a much more powerful opponent could in certain circumstances be effective as a deterrent to that opponent. Although there are many technical problems involved, a nation possessing only a small number of nuclear weapons, together with their means of delivery, may be able to inflict damage on a far better equipped nation which that nation would consider unacceptable. Such was not the case with conventional weapons, where the ratio between the size and effectiveness of a given force was far smaller. Economic and technical factors had prevented any nation except the United States, the Soviet Union and Great Britain from developing a nuclear force earlier. By the early 1960s, however, independent nuclear capacity of a rudimentary nature was already possessed by France (1960) and China (1964), while a number of other countries were in a position to tread the same path if they were prepared to undertake the considerable expenditure required.

Among the countries that could be classified in this group were two European 'traditional' neutrals, Switzerland and Sweden. Especially in the case of Switzerland, the argument for an independent nuclear deterrent follows logically from the nation's long-standing reliance on the highest degree of armed preparedness as the best guarantee of its neutrality. One writer has called this 'belligerent neutrality'.[14]

Thus the 1960s have seen a modification of the rationale of

neutralism because of the trend towards polycentrism and the not unrelated doctrine of the independent nuclear deterrent. If there can be local wars on a considerable scale to which the cold war (if indeed that term still has any real application) is wholly or partly irrelevant, then deterrence necessarily assumes greater significance for a neutralist power than it did a decade earlier. If possession of an independent nuclear deterrent is feasible for a number of countries, then a far more active and independent foreign policy may be possible for certain neutralist nations whose initiatives in foreign policy have previously been restricted.

The techniques of infiltration and guerrilla warfare practised by the Viet Cong in Vietnam form in their effectiveness a curious parallel to the theory of the independent deterrent. In both cases the possessor of overwhelming nuclear capacity is hamstrung by its inability to deal effectively with a seemingly far weaker weapon in the hands of its puny adversary. The Vietnam war has, indeed, served to delay the end of the cold war by prolonging the estrangement between the United States and the Soviet Union, but it has not halted the trend towards polycentrism. In these circumstances the future prospects for neutralism seem quite bright. Its characteristics, however, may well be closer to those of traditional neutrality than to the theories of Nehru.

Successive Japanese conservative governments have rejected neutralism as an 'illusion'. (The term was popularized by Prime Minister Ikeda during the 1960 election campaign.) In terms of the distinction made above, they have both cherished a preference and also taken sides. Neutralism stands rejected on both these counts. The United States has been Japan's military protector and chief trading partner, while enjoying official Japanese support on a variety of world issues. (Also, for what it is worth, America has consistently figured as the 'least disliked country' in Japanese public opinion polls.)[15] Relations between the two countries have of course had their ups and downs, and in June 1960 reached their nadir when President Eisenhower's projected visit to Japan had to be cancelled because of anticipated riots. Nevertheless both mutual self-interest and compatible ideologies have usually persuaded the two governments to co-operate on essentials.

It is indeed pertinent to ask whether, in the early 1950s at any rate, a foreign policy radically different from that actually pursued would have been for Japan a practical proposition. The country was weak and demoralized, though rapidly recovering. The legacy of the American Occupation was still strong, and included a substantial military presence. It would have been an extraordinarily bold (or fanatical) government that dared to repudiate at that time the American connection. The defence argument also loomed large. Japan during the Korean war had minimal armed forces of her own, and while an outright Soviet or Chinese invasion was hardly likely, the opportunities for blackmail no doubt seemed considerable. Japan's cities, as had been amply proved in 1945, were vulnerable to air attack. In the circumstances the Yoshida government had little hesitation in striking a bargain with the Americans for military protection.

The contrast with India is instructive. To Nehru the need for defence against foreign communist attack seemed less pressing, partly because of geography and partly because of his own general outlook on world politics. There had been no American occupation of India as there had been of a defeated Japan, and so no question arose of simply continuing in a modified form existing military arrangements. Perhaps most important, Nehru saw the opportunities which non-alignment presented for the performance by India of an active role in world affairs. Japan, who in 1950 was little liked and less understood in the capitals of Asia, could scarcely have aspired to such an international position. Certainly the pressures for Japan's participation in cold war politics were far stronger than they were for India.

In one respect, however, the two countries were not entirely dissimilar. Both had gone through periods of anti-western nationalism. The relevance of this for Indian neutralism has already been remarked.

Japan had never herself been a colony, but neither had she been free from the agony of feeling inferior to western powers. Her leaders of the late nineteenth century sought to industrialize with utmost despatch specifically in order to extricate Japan from the semi-colonial position which western countries had forced upon her. Thereafter her governmental structure was precariously poised between a number of competing élites, one of which was the top echelons of the armed forces. By the late 1920s a slight shift in the character of this balance made it possible for the armed forces to gain the upper hand, while within the army itself rabidly chauvinistic doctrines came to the fore. This type of nationalism led in the end to a physically and psychologically crushing military defeat.

The next five and a half years of foreign occupation were unique in her history. American rule was unexpectedly enlightened and was governed, in part at least, by a zeal for social and political reform. Nevertheless, once the Occupation ended the inevitable nationalist reaction set in. This time, however, it was expressed not by the army (which had been disbanded) nor by ultra-rightist gangs (which were thoroughly discredited) but principally by the left. There was a complex of reasons for this. In part, it was because of a fundamental shift of policy by the Occupation in its later stages. The initial programme was in many ways favourable to (and was welcomed by) the forces of the left wing. This was particularly true with labour legislation, which breathed new life into the stunted trade union movement. Democratization of the political structure, the purge of conservative politicians, and anti-trust legislation all encouraged the growth of socialism. Perhaps the most momentous reform, in terms of its effect on the left wing, was article 9 (the 'pacifist clause') of the new Constitution, a document in which American ideas and influence predominated. Article 9 read as follows:

> Aspiring sincerely to an international peace based on justice and order, the Japanese people forever renounce war as a sovereign right of the nation and the threat or use of force as a means of settling international disputes.
> In order to accomplish the aim of the preceding paragraph, land, sea and air forces, as well as other war potential, will never be maintained. The right of belligerency of the state will not be recognized.

The spirit of this article proved congenial to many Japanese socialists, although, as we shall see later, they became most vigorous in its defence only after the Americans themselves had begun to entertain serious doubts about its wisdom. The policies of the later years of the Occupation were much less favourable to labour than the earlier period, as the Americans threw their weight behind Japan under a conservative administration as an anti-communist bastion. As the Americans cracked down on left wing trade unions, while simultaneously urging the Japanese to reconsider rearmament, the rising streams of socialism and pacifism flowed together into an anti-American torrent. When the Occupation ended but American military bases and troops remained on Japanese soil in substantial numbers, slogans about 'American imperialism' became (and remained) the stock-in-trade of the most dynamic and successful socialist factions. The neutralist programme that these factions developed owed much to an essentially nationalist feeling of curtailed sovereignty, expressed in terms of a certain Marxist tradition which itself contained nationalist elements.

If, however, the left wing had 'captured' the nationalist movement in Japan, its form and content were very different from the nationalism that had flourished as a right wing protest movement in the 1930s. As one western scholar put it: 'a Suzuki Mosaburō [the leading Marxist socialist during the 1950s] cannot intone the slogans of "racial" or "national" unity with the same conviction as an old-style fire-eating nationalist of prewar days.'[16] One might add that around 1950 this same Suzuki coined an election slogan of great appeal to the war-weary Japanese: 'Youth of Japan! Never again let it be your lot to take up arms!'[17] Pacifism, indeed, would seem to be the very antithesis of nationalism. Yet even pacifism had here a decided nationalist content. A permanently disarmed Japan was put forward by the left as the essential means of preventing 'rearmament on behalf of the United States'.[18] More subtly, it was also advanced as a unique contribution which Japan could present to the world.[19] In Japan of the 1950s, this added up to a powerful and cohesive doctrine, often embarrassing to the government of the day. Where socialists were campaigning against American bases in Japan, or American administration of Okinawa, or the creeping rearmament of Japan which was being conducted in defiance of the spirit if not the letter of the Constitution, or revision (seen as perpetuation) of the Security Treaty between the United States and Japan of 8 September 1951, then Marxists, pacifists and nationalists could sit together quite comfortably on the same platform. There were occasions when straight-forwardly nationalist issues such as Japanese attempts to secure the return of territory from the Soviet Union, placed socialists in something of a dilemma. Should they support the maximum Japanese territorial claim at the expense of better overall relations with the Soviet Union or should they sacrifice the possibility of better relations on the altar of territorial intransigence? Generally speaking right wing socialists opted for the latter alternative, while left wing socialists opted for the former.[20]

It would, however, be misleading to interpret neutralism in Japan wholly in nationalist terms, powerful though this motivation has been. The doubts repeatedly expressed by Japanese left wing politicians and by many intellectuals about the worth of America's pledge to guarantee Japan's security have been sincerely held and are worth treating seriously on their merits.[21] Too often, the fact that such views have been expressed in phrases echoing Marxist ideology has been taken in the west as evidence that the views themselves are either hopelessly doctrinaire or else disingenuous. The lack of electoral success by the JSP in recent years has lent weight to this dismissive attitude. Nevertheless, pragmatic political analysis often lies not far below the surface of much thinking on foreign policy within the party, despite the ideological language in which party pronouncements are frequently shrouded. Moreover many of the assumptions of this thinking about Japan's role in world politics have increasingly much in common with the views of the left wing factions of the ruling LDP.

There is something remarkably 'Gaullist' about the neutralist arguments of Japanese socialists, although it is a 'Gaullism' modified by the absence of the concept of an independent nuclear deterrent. Even here, however, the situation seems to have within it elements of fluidity, since the present party leaders have shown themselves ambivalent, to say the least, about the question of preventing nuclear proliferation. It is essential to remember that the main aim of JSP neutralism has in practice been to terminate the Security Treaty. All other campaigns which the party has waged are far less significant, in the party's own estimation, than the campaign to secure 'true' independence from the United States.

In this connection two arguments have been consistently advanced. One is that the Security Treaty does not give to Japan an effective safeguard of her security because there is no reason for confidence that the defence of Japan is uppermost in the minds of American leaders responsible for implementing the Treaty. The other is that the severance of Japan's defence ties with the United States would not adversely affect stability in Asia or the Pacific.

Japanese neutralism has rested on a thorough distrust both of the motives of American policy toward Japan and of the validity of the strategic premises upon which the Security Treaty was ostensibly founded. The JSP has always emphasized the instability of mutual nuclear deterrence, believing that the danger of provoking a nuclear attack upon Japan far outweighed any possible contribution to a global balance which Japan's alliance with the United States might make. While agreeing that even a neutralist Japan would be unlikely to escape destruction in an all-out nuclear war, they have argued that the presence of American troops and bases in Japan and Okinawa was as likely to provoke the Soviet Union into a pre-emptive nuclear attack as to serve as genuine deterrence or protection. According to one left wing writer at least, the presumed fact (often doubted, incidentally, by the JSP) that there were no nuclear warheads on Japanese soil could be of little comfort to Japan. The very possibility of their presence being suspected by the Soviet Union could well be sufficient excuse for an attack by the latter.[22] Others have emphasized the speed with which nuclear warheads could physically be brought into Japan by the Americans in case of a major international crisis, and have pointed out that in modern war signal and supply bases might well be prime objectives of nuclear attack.[23] The fact that in 1958–60 Prime Minister Kishi himself fought hard and successfully to have inserted into the revised Security Treaty a 'prior consultation' clause (which everyone knew was chiefly aimed to give the Japanese side some means of preventing the American introduction of nuclear weapons into Japan) suggests that the government was also not unconcerned with this kind of danger.

Thus the Security Treaty for the socialists has represented not deterrence but 'provocation'.[24] There is, however, another side to their argument, namely that the Treaty, as such, is quite unnecessary. The only neighbouring countries conceivably capable of attacking Japan are the Soviet Union and communist China. The Soviet Union would not, they argue, launch an attack except as part of some general conflagration. China's manufacture of nuclear weapons has not produced a particularly strong reaction in Japan generally, and the JSP as yet gives no sign of thinking that China is a potential problem for Japan's security. (This is not to say that China's bomb does not present a considerable moral and political problem for the party.)

One effect of polycentric trends in world affairs in recent years has been to undermine part of the original rationale of neutralism in Japan. It is now no longer necessary to work for an end to the all-pervading Soviet-American confrontation, seen as an ever-present danger to the peace of the world although Vietnam has produced similar fears about Chinese-American relations. Japan herself is in a more complex international environment than she was in the early 1950s and is also herself a much more important factor in that environment. At the same time the efficacy and desirability, in its present form, of the Mutual Security Treaty which was drawn up while the Soviet-American confrontation still dominated world affairs, is still the subject of much critical discussion in Japan. It is an open question whether the Treaty will continue as it is for long after 1970— the date from which either side may, giving one year's notice, call for its renegotiation or rescission—whatever government may be in power in Tokyo.[25]

Whether the JSP's neutralist doctrines are likely to develop even further along the lines of Gaullism is very difficult to predict. Scarcely anybody associated with the party has ever advocated armed neutralism,[26] and nuclear neutralism would run counter to the pacifist and anti-nuclear sentiments which lie deep in the party's heritage. On the other hand, as in West Germany, the post-war reaction against a militarist past is slowly giving way to a reassertion of national pride and self-confidence. In this writer's view, the chances of the Japanese socialists being won round to supporting an independent Japanese nuclear force are not great within the next five to ten years. The likelihood, however, of some sort of a foreign policy consensus developing between the left wing parties and some sections at least of the LDP seems more considerable. This might well be premised on the loosening of ties with the United States and a more self-reliant, positive approach to international problems.

It is hoped that the following description and analysis will help the reader to form his own judgments on these questions with greater confidence.

2

THE JSP AND ITS LEGACY
FROM THE PAST

Since the early 1950s Japanese socialism has been closely connected with neutralism. Although, however, neutralism was a product of the post-war world, socialism had already sunk a few hardy roots deep into the uncongenial soil of Imperial Japan. The post-war JSP leaders had behind them in most cases two or three decades of political experience. They had not called themselves neutralists before, but had often had to formulate attitudes to vital foreign policy problems, including those of war and militarism. Nor was their store of political experience confined to matters of policy. Factional differences, normally related to ideology but sometimes more fundamentally concerned with questions of personal loyalty and interpersonal rivalry, had become apparent from an early stage in the Japanese socialist movement. These differences were largely carried over intact to the post-war period, and profoundly influenced the nature and course of the party's foreign policy.

Post-war socialist leadership is easily divided into three 'generations', the first consisting of those who participated in radical movements at the turn of the twentieth century, the second being socialist activists of the 1920s, and the third, men who entered the left wing movement after World War II. In the decade of Japanese socialism following 1950, by far the most important of these 'generations' was the second.[1]

The JSP, from its inauguration in 1945, consisted of three main factions, whose leaders were all of the second 'generation'. Each of these factions took a different view of the problems of Japan's foreign policy in the 1950s. A right wing faction, though very critical of certain aspects of Japan's alliance with the

United States, generally supported the principle behind it, that of security against communism through American military help. At the other extreme, a left wing faction was the chief sponsor of the policy of neutralism, the immediate aims of which were the renunciation of all military ties with the United States, the abolition of indigenous armed forces and the cultivation of closer relations with (though not, it hoped, dependence upon) the Soviet Union and communist China. Third, there was a centre faction, which in certain periods leaned towards the foreign policy of the right wing faction and in other periods towards that of the left wing faction, maintaining in general less internal cohesion and intellectual consistency than either of the other two.

These three factions were, both in personnel and ideology, a continuation of three separate political parties into which the Japanese socialist movement split in 1926.[2]

One most important factor which distinguished them was that after 1931 the left wing faction alone of socialist groups resolutely and consistently opposed Japan's drift into militarist government and foreign aggression. Its 'unblemished' record in this regard explains to some extent the power which it was able to gain within the JSP in the atmosphere of revulsion from war which prevailed after 1945. Significantly, it was this left wing faction that took the initiative in introducing neutralism to the party. Why this should have been so will be discussed later.

First, however, it is important to see why this faction resisted the militarists while others trimmed their sails to the prevailing wind.

Antipathy to the militarist outlook of the Japanese State can be traced back to protests by some radicals and socialists against the Russo-Japanese war of 1904–6. Their protests derived from three sources: Christian pacifism, the Marxist view that war was a product of imperialism, and theories of 'proletarian internationalism'.[3]

When in 1914 the German Social-Democratic Party told its supporters to back the Kaiser's war, 'proletarian internationalism' lay in ruins. The failure of social democrats of different countries to unite in opposing a nationalist war paved the way for the split in the Second International. In Japan, as elsewhere, the gap between socialists of the left (including communists) and those of the centre and right was consequently wide.

The Marxist left eagerly assimilated Leninist doctrine that wars resulted from the imperialism of capitalist governments: therefore if Japan went to war, Japanese socialists should oppose their government's action. (Right wing and moderate socialists, on the other hand, were in a more equivocal position. Since their attitude was not purely Marxist, they did not find it easy to decide how to treat Japan's external aggression during the 1930s. To some extent the appeal of nationalism, and of the slogan *'foreign* imperialism', affected them as it had affected the German Social-Democratic Party in 1914.)

The platforms of the various socialist parties formed after 1925 said little about war, armaments or militarism, and it is scarcely possible to distinguish left from right by the way in which these problems were treated.[4] No doubt they had to be cautious in the face of government persecution. However, after the 1931 Japanese army coup in Manchuria (known as the Manchurian 'Incident') only the left wing faction consistently opposed the militarists and their overseas exploits.[5] In July 1932 the pressure of international events impelled the various socialist groups (except one band of 'National Socialists' inspired by Hitler) to combine in a single party, the *Shakai Taishūtō* (Social Masses Party) which, as we shall see, moved ever closer to the militarists. In 1937 the left wing faction, in disgust at this trend, broke away to form its own party opposed to militarism and war. This move, which was influenced by the current idea of a 'Popular Front' against nazism and fascism, ended in the arrest of four hundred participants.

The communists, too, protested against war and imperialism. They, however, laboured under peculiar difficulties. Communist parties had twice been formed (in 1922 and 1926) and on each occasion quickly suppressed. There were mass arrests, particularly in 1929, which reduced communism in the 1930s to a negligible force. What was important in retrospect, however, was the legacy of an ideological dispute between communists and left wing socialists. These two groups had conducted a prolonged and bitter debate about the strategy of revolution, which profoundly influenced their respective views on revolutionary strategy and hence foreign policy after World War II. In 1926 an intellectual study group (*Rōnō-ha*) associated with the left wing faction was formed by Yamakawa Hitoshi (who had participated in the founding of the communist party of 1922, but later seceded). This group has ever since remained a vital influence on the left wing of the JSP.[6]

The late 1920s dispute between the *Rōnō-ha* and the *Kōza-ha* (as the group taking the communist line was called) brings us back to our earlier question: why did the left wing faction, whose pre-war anti-militarist record enabled it to attain a dominant position in the JSP after World War II, come to pioneer a neutralist foreign policy?

There is little doubt that the *Rōnō-ha* view of revolutionary strategy strongly affected post-war Left Socialist foreign policy attitudes. First, however, it is important to see what the *Rōnō-ha* was originally attacking. The *Kōza-ha* maintained that in Japan 'feudal elements' (including the emperor) still predominated in the organs of state, which had been seized by a combination of large-scale landowners and the commercial bourgeoisie. A two-stage revolution was therefore necessary: the first, or 'bourgeois-democratic' stage was needed to overthrow these vestiges of a feudal age; only after that had been successfully accomplished could the 'proletarian-socialist' stage of the revolution take place.[7]

The *Rōnō-ha*, on the other hand, argued that Japan was at an 'advanced' capitalist stage of development. Thus it followed, in Marxist thinking, that revolutionary strategy appropriate for 'advanced' societies should be pursued. This was a one-stage 'proletarian-socialist' revolution omitting the prior 'bourgeois-democratic' stage.[8]

In the early 1950s Left Socialists and communists were still to a great extent under the spell of the *Rōnō-Kōza* dispute. Since the *Kōza-ha* had considered Japan a 'backward' country (dialectically speaking) the Japan Communist Party (JCP), even after the Peace Treaty came into force in 1952, often called her a 'colony' of the United States. This was a status reminiscent for Marxists of pre-1949 China. Left Socialists, on the other hand, applying the *Rōnō-ha* principle that Japan had reached an 'advanced' stage of capitalism, thought essentially that Japan was able to stand on her own feet in relations with the United States. In one sense, the neutralism of the Left Socialists was *less* nationalistic than was communist foreign poicy. It was not so strident in its anti-Americanism and sought, while loosening existing ties with the United States, to maintain relations with that country 'on the basis of equality', rather than entering the camp of her 'enemies'. In another sense their neutralism was *more* nationalistic than the policies of the JCP. Believing Japan to be an advanced country, they came increasingly to think that her foreign policy should be that of a 'Great Power' and not of a backward country.

We must now turn to the compromise with militarism made by many socialists (other than those of the left wing) during the 1930s.

The evidence suggests that socialist collusion with the militarists, although to some extent unavoidable in the circumstances, sprang partly from a genuine chauvinism and also from a certain attraction exercised by 'direct' rather than parliamentary method. Again, such attitudes influenced the approach to neutralism made by these same socialists after World War II.

A distinction must be made between the right wing faction and the centre faction, since the former was never committed to the militarists to the extent that was true of the latter. Indeed, the two came into conflict in the late 1930s.[9] The right wing faction consistently supported parliamentary government and opposed extreme solutions to the nation's ills. After World War II it was generally pro-western and anti-neutralist. The centre faction, on the other hand, bore the main responsibility for leading the *Shakai Taishūtō* during the 1930s into support for militarism. In the 1950s its attitudes to foreign policy were equivocal, hovering between pro-western and neutralist. This can be explained in part by the discredit into which the faction was brought within the JSP as a result of its pre-war policies, and its consequent uncertainty about which direction to take. In so far, however, as it supported neutralism, this seems to have been for reasons not unconnected with its pre-war chauvinism.

The appeal of ultra-nationalist creeds to pre-war socialists is a fascinating subject for study, and is relevant to their post-war views. In Japan the roots of nationalism were deep, and from the Meiji period the mechanism of nationalist appeal had both disciplined and galvanized the energies of the people. With the great depression of the 1930s nationalism became an essentially revolutionary creed led by young military officers and supported by a depressed peasantry.

In the general election of 1932 the socialist parties between them only elected five members to the Diet. This was a clear sign that they had lost the initiative in a potentially revolutionary situation. As a consequence some socialists were persuaded that by jumping onto the militarist bandwagon they might be able to capture a revolutionary movement which looked like being successful. This trend was reinforced by governmental pressure on the socialist movement during the 1930s.

There was an important long-standing division between those socialists who wished to attain socialism within the legal confines of the parliamentary system, and those who believed that revolution could not be achieved without 'direct action' on the part of the masses leading to the violent overthrow of the government.

This conflict was evident even in the first 'generation' of Japanese socialists. At the time of the Russo-Japanese war the parliamentary and reformist wing of the movement, dedicated among other things to the achievement of universal suffrage, was predominant. In 1906, however, a leading radical, Kōtoku Denjirō, returned from the United States imbued with anarchist ideas, and a controversy ensued within the radical movement between his followers, advocating 'direct action', and those who supported parliamentarism and legality.

The extremist approach to 'direct action', which gained ground among socialists and radicals between 1906 and the trial and execution of Kōtoku for his alleged part in the anarchist plot of 1910 to assassinate the Emperor, was similar to that of extremist right wing malcontents who supported nationalist causes by resort to violence. That there was some overlap between the extreme left and the extreme right in method if not in ultimate aims is shown by the brief existence of a state socialist party (*Kokka Shakaitō*) dedicated to Japan's 'national polity' (a powerful nationalist slogan) and also to social betterment.

The second 'generation' leaders of socialism in Japan began their careers at the height of the period known as 'Taishō Democracy', when democratic and parliamentary forms possessed for the first time some real significance. These same leaders, however, before long had to face a formidable challenge from the ideology of militarism. In order to gain some understanding of their response, we shall look at two key leaders who later sided with the militarists. The first, Akamatsu Katsumaro, founded a national socialist party in 1932; the second, Asō Hisashi, more gradually led the *Shakai Taishūtō* into conformity with the nationalist creed.[10]

Between 1922 and 1932 Akamatsu Katsumaro progressed from communism, through right wing social democracy to national socialism. Having graduated from Tokyo Imperial University in 1919, where he was a leading member of a formative socialist study group, the *Shinjinkai* (New Man Society), he entered labour politics and in 1922 joined the first Japanese communist party. In response to arrests of communists during 1923 the party debated whether to dissolve. Akamatsu led the advocates of dissolution, and in February 1924 the party decided that this would be the best course. At the same time Akamatsu announced that he now thought it would be better to co-operate to some extent with the government, whose policies at that time were relatively liberal and culminated in the grant of manhood suffrage in 1925. He gave three 'objective social conditions' as reasons for his change of course: the current stabilization of capitalism, the low ebb in the fortunes of the Third International, and the progress of democracy in Japan.[11]

Consequently, in 1926, when the socialist movement split into left, centre and right wings, Akamatsu entered the right wing party. After leaving the communist party he argued that socialism might be attained in different ways, and this may have foreshadowed his later development as a nationalist. He adumbrated a theory which he called 'scientific Japanism' (*Kagakuteki Nihonshugi*). In 1924 he wrote:

Each country has different conditions, leading to different ways of getting to socialism. Besides the universal rules of social progress, we must also know the Japanese nation. A true scientific proletarian class leadership policy for Japan must be contrived.[12]

Akamatsu remained a right wing socialist until the Manchurian 'Incident' of 1931 which brought about a further change in his thinking.

At the January 1932 Congress of the right wing party, the first after the Manchurian 'Incident', Akamatsu sponsored a controversial statement of basic policy which ran as follows:

(1) We proclaim our spirit of respect for Japan's national polity.

(2) In recognition of the essence of the State, we reject the Marxist view of the State as an oppressor, and proclaim that we support a view of the State as an organ of true controlling capacity, and we aim at giving this controlling capacity a mass character.

(3) In a world situation of bitter national struggle, we proclaim that Marxist internationalism, which ignores national interests and upholds only the joint interests of the proletariat as a whole, and aims at a single mechanical international struggle, is empty and mistaken, and we accept a more realistic internationalism which proclaims the national position of the proletariat.

(4) Hitherto we have not thought that parliamentarism was the solution for everything, but we have opposed the Communist Party which totally rejected parliamentarism, and our Action Policy has gradually come to give the impression that we did see parliamentarism as the solution to all problems. We now think that it is necessary to get rid of this impression, and facing the present objective situation, we recognize that alongside parliamentary policies, it is necessary to develop a lively mass movement outside the Diet.[13]

This statement precipitated a split in the right wing party and the founding of Akamatsu's own party of National Socialists. Throughout the 1930s he became increasingly committed to the militarists.

Like Akamatsu, Asō Hisashi was a leading member of the *Shinjinkai* at the end of World War I, and was similarly influenced by its vague romanticism derived from the Russian Populists whose ideal was for intellectuals to plunge into the sordid life of the masses.[14] The *Shinjinkai* fostered a wide cross-section of the leaders of the proletarian movements which organized political parties after 1926, and among these were some who later became dedicated Marxists. Asō, on the other hand, though much influenced by Marxism and by the Russian revolution, did not become a Marxist in the same sense. He was said to have held an unusual view of the significance of the Russian revolution, believing that Lenin derived more of his thought from 'Mother Russia' than from Marxism; in other words that Lenin fundamentally understood the Russian people. Asō therefore held that socialists in Japan must in a similar way understand the Japanese.[15]

In the Socialist split of 1926, Asō led the centre party. His principal aim between 1926 and 1932 was to unite the fissiparous socialist movement into one party which should be capable of revolution. Although he was not of the Marxist left, his earnest belief in revolution distinguished him less from the left than from the right.

Asō's conversion to support for the militarists took place later than that of Akamatsu. His immediate reaction to the Manchurian 'Incident' was to condemn the Japanese action: 'The imperialist policy taken towards our neighbour China by the government and the military could well lead to a world war, and we therefore oppose it resolutely.'[16] We may date his conversion from October 1934, in his reaction to a series of pamphlets prepared by the Army Ministry calling for increased armaments spending. The following statement is particularly revealing:

> The pamphlets clearly recognize that capitalism, which sacrifices the whole proletariat for its own selfish interest, and which amidst all misunderstanding we shall fight to the death, does not contribute to true national development. They see in Japan's national situation, and the social reformation required to overthrow capitalism, the necessity for rational unity between the armed forces and the proletariat.

The only way to achieve this aim is strictly to implement this unity. These pamphlets have officially laid open this way. Just to fear military uniforms is a delusion of a liberal age.[17]

As this statement shows, Asō was concerned to join forces with the militarists if possible. He almost certainly wished thus to borrow the strength of a powerful and, in his opinion, potentially revolutionary force, the military, and thus to reinforce the weakness of existing socialism. Doubts have been expressed by those with the advantage of hindsight about the sanity of such an enterprise,[18] but the explanation is probably that given by Kawakami Tamio, whose opinion can be summarized as follows: that after World War II Asō was posthumously criticized as having betrayed socialism, which was indeed true, but he had not betrayed his own beliefs. His guiding principle (retained from the *Shinjinkai* period) was his desire to see a revolution in his lifetime.[19] After the 1929 crash and the world depression, he believed that the catastrophic fall of capitalism was at hand; socialism in Japan, however, was still weak, and therefore he thought that an effort should be made to split the ruling class by alliance with the militarists.[20] Undoubtedly another reason, as argued by a writer who was closely associated with Asō, was that the *Shakai Taishūtō* was forced to take increasingly nationalistic positions during the 1930s for the sake of self-preservation.[21] Nevertheless, the evidence suggests that the adjustment was not made entirely unwillingly.

Our comparison of Akamatsu and Asō suggests two important characteristics possessed in common by pre-war socialists attracted to ultra-nationalism: first, a conviction that the uniqueness of Japan must in some sense modify the universal character of Marxism; second, a preference for 'direct action' as a means to goal-attainment, and rejection of parliamentarism as the sole channel for reform. This could of course be said about an even wider range of socialists than those who made overtures to the militarists. A feeling for the uniqueness of Japan did not necessarily make them into aggressive chauvinists.

Pre-war socialist experience is relevant to post-war JSP foreign policy because of the persistence of these factors despite the intervention of revolutionary changes in Japan, and to some extent new aims for the socialist movement itself. Important effects of Japan's defeat in World War II were a reaction against the war and the popularity of pacifism. Those socialist factions whose desire for revolution had led them to support the militarists were discredited and their influence reduced. Those that had stood out against them survived the war with their reputation greatly enhanced. Nevertheless, the American presence in the post-war period provided scope for the re-emergence of a kind of nationalism, and to some extent of the 'direct action' that had traditionally accompanied it. The result (discussed later) was a pacifist, but revolutionary and anti-foreign, neutralism.

3

THE JSP ADOPTS
'PERMANENT NEUTRALITY'

In December 1949 the JSP officially adopted a foreign policy of 'permanent neutrality'. It was introduced in the following terms:

> Japan ought in no circumstances to contemplate the possibility of a peace treaty with less than all the powers that fought against Japan . . . Our party, having regard to the neutral status established by the Constitution, opposes the conclusion of any military or political agreement with a particular country or a particular group of countries.[1]

This was the first official commitment of the JSP to neutrality or neutralism in foreign affairs. Its essence was later embodied in the 'three peace principles'. These were: (a) a peace treaty with all the belligerent powers; (b) permanent neutrality; (c) no military bases to be given to a foreign power.

The fact that such a policy was not adopted earlier by the JSP may be explained on a superficial level by its preoccupation with questions other than foreign affairs. Japan was engaged in post-war reconstruction and was implementing the democratic reforms of the Occupation. The socialists were building up a labour movement with their newly found freedom of organization, and were struggling to keep control of the trade unions out of the hands of the communists. Moreover, Japan, under the Occupation, was not in a position to conduct her own diplomacy, and her security was guaranteed, at any rate for the time being, by the presence of Allied forces. Thus socialists had little reason to discuss at length questions of future Japanese external relations, and few references were made to such questions in socialist publications before 1949.

Nevertheless, the adoption of 'permanent neutrality' was not merely resumption of a previous policy, but a significant new departure in socialist thinking on foreign affairs. This was caused by a much altered international environment, and by a shift in the balance of power between factions in the JSP itself.

For several months preceding the JSP policy statement, neutrality (in the pre-war sense) was publicly discussed in a number of quarters. In April 1949 it received some support (though not from the JSP) in an Upper House Diet debate.[2] In the academic world neutrality was aired in a lengthy published debate (discussed in chapter 11) between two eminent international lawyers, one of whom advocated permanent neutrality, while the other rejected it as incompatible with 'collective security' under the UN. Some measure of agreement on the desirability of neutrality was reached by a brilliant and well-publicized university group, the *Heiwa Mondai Danwakai* (Discussion Circle on Problems of Peace).[3]

It was commonly realized that Japan would soon have to make decisions about defence, in a world becoming increasingly troubled. This caused in many cases a strong anti-war reaction.

Public debate was prompted not so much by Soviet-American tension in Europe as by some American statements about the future status of Japan. In February 1949 the United States Secretary for War, Mr K. C. Royall, was quoted as saying that he considered Japan strategically less important than Europe, so that in a large-scale war the United States might not attempt to defend her.[4] Despite an official denial, this report fostered the suspicion that a change had taken place in American policy, perhaps heralding an imminent withdrawal of Allied forces. At least one leading newspaper commented editorially that since apparently it was no longer possible to rely on American protection, Japan should seek an early peace treaty at which she should obtain an international guarantee of neutrality.[5]

This argument gained support from an interview given by General MacArthur to a British correspondent in March 1949. MacArthur was reported as saying that the United States never intended to use Japan as an ally and did not want her to fight. She should remain neutral, and her role was to become the

Switzerland of the Pacific.[6] These words also produced a press reaction in favour of neutrality.

American support for Japanese neutrality did not, however, long outlast the victory of the communist revolution in China. On 5 November 1949 a report was 'leaked' from Occupation Headquarters that General MacArthur hoped for an early peace treaty. He thought that the Soviet Union and communist China should be present at the peace conference but without a veto, and that the security of Japan would probably require the continued presence of American forces, with their existing bases.[7] A month later the JSP adopted 'permanent neutrality' as its foreign policy.

Before looking at the connection between American policy and the new JSP line let us contrast it with immediate post-war socialist attitudes to foreign policy. This will indicate how far the new line differed from previous socialist thinking.

In 1945 the JSP rejected the chauvinistic policies of pre-war socialism. In this it shared a common reaction against the men who had led Japan into war. The party's first Congress in November agreed without difficulty on three guiding principles. The third of these (the first two expressed the aims of democracy and socialism respectively) read: 'Our party opposes all militaristic thought and action, and aims at the realization of perpetual peace through the co-operation of the peoples of the world.'[8]

In the 1946 Lower House Diet debates on the new Constitution containing the 'pacifist clause' the JSP voted unanimously in favour of the final draft, thus distinguishing itself from six Communists and two independents who alone voted against it. In the course of debate the JSP Chairman, Katayama Tetsu, backed the pacifist clause saying that it should be strengthened with a declaration of devotion to world peace.[9] Subsequent party policy statements harped on this pacifist theme and attacked Japan's imperialist past: although they called for an early peace treaty, the question of national defence after independence was rarely mentioned. The few references to the subject appealed to the UN as the guarantor of collective security on a world scale.[10]

There is in fact no evidence that before 1949 neutrality was ever seriously considered within the JSP as a post-independence policy for Japan. Moreover, during the Diet debates on the Constitution one socialist specifically rejected the 'anachronism' of neutrality *à la suisse*, as proposed by a member of the Liberal Party. He warned that this would be to invite foreign nations to fight their wars on Japanese soil, an eventuality that could only be prevented if Japan were admitted to the UN and were able to conclude security treaties.[11]

The contrast between these views and the policy adopted by the JSP at the end of 1949 was partly the result of a changed international perspective. 'Progressive' opinion on international affairs in 1946 was influenced by the still recent experience of a total war which led many people to doubt whether neutrality was either ethical or practicable. At this stage, also, the ideal of the UN as an all-powerful international peacekeeper was still strong. By late 1949, on the other hand, the United States and the Soviet Union had already begun their cold war, and the former was seeking allies in order to prevent further gains by the latter. The victory of the communists in China brought this confrontation to the Far East. The discrepancy between the statements of American authorities in early and in late 1949 (mentioned above) laid American policy open to the accusation that her only interest in Japan was the creation of a base against the further spread of communism in the Far East. The fear expressed by a socialist in 1946 that a neutral Japan might be turned into a battleground in a war between foreigners was thus projected into the situation of a possible anti-communist pact with the United States.

The rationale of a neutralist Japan was set out by a leading socialist, Suzuki Mosaburō, in the official socialist newspaper in October 1949. Suzuki said that the low American estimate of Japan's strategic importance to her had been revised by the revolution in China. The Americans were therefore trying to build up Japan (and India) as anti-communist strongholds. Japan, however, rather than becoming America's ally against China, should seek to 'consolidate Japan's economic self-reliance and independence within world peace and friendship, as Nehru is doing in India'. Japan need not fear China, which could not do without Japanese trade and aid for her industrialization programme.[12]

This article highlighted two themes which recurred frequently in later socialist foreign policy: a desire to opt out of American plans for Japan as an anti-communist bastion (with all that was thought to imply in terms of loss of independence and possible involvement in war) and a belief in the interdependence of Japan and China irrespective of the régime in the latter. The influence of Indian neutralism was already evident. In both cases the principal aim (outweighing any apprehension about communism) was to escape involvement in the American power bloc.

Thus the world situation in 1949 was one major reason why the JSP embarked on its neutralist career. Its choice, however, was also influenced by more parochial factors, in particular a shift to the left in the party itself. Four factions helped to found the JSP in 1945. Of these, one seceded in 1948, leaving three called (after their post-war leaders) the Nishio faction (right wing), the Kawakami faction (centre) and the Suzuki faction (left wing).

In 1947–8 the JSP participated (with two other parties) in a coalition cabinet and for the first time in history a Socialist, Katayama Tetsu, was Prime Minister of Japan. Never before had the party undertaken the burdens of ministerial office, and in retrospect it is obvious that the experience was disastrously premature. The party (and indeed the coalition government as a whole) was dominated by the strongly anti-communist Nishio faction of which Katayama was a member. A condition of the coalition agreement was that the left wing Suzuki faction should be excluded from the cabinet, and withdrawal of this faction's support in February 1948 finally caused the government to fall. The socialists had a few more months in office in a reconstructed cabinet under a non-socialist Prime Minister, but this government also expired, amid financial scandals, in October of the same year.[13] The weakness and poor record of these cabinets discredited the JSP in the eyes of the electorate. The party was routed in the Lower House general election of January 1949, in which its share of Diet seats fell from 143 to 48. This marked the end of right wing dominance of the JSP. At the party Congress of April 1949 the Suzuki faction for the first time won the Secretary-Generalship for its leader, Suzuki Mosaburō. From there on the left wing had the upper hand, although the right wing and centre factions continued to fight stubborn rear-guard actions.[14]

An important reason why the JSP took up with neutralist ideas at the end of 1949 was that the leadership of the party had passed to the Suzuki faction. Although no evidence is available whether any division of opinion occurred in the Central Executive Committee before the party policy statement of 10 December 1949, it is clear that the main advocates of neutrality were from the Suzuki faction, while the Nishio faction seems to have been already most unhappy with the idea.[15] Confirmation of this last point is to be found in the memoirs of the greatest of Japan's post-war prime ministers, Yoshida Shigeru. According to Yoshida, in 1947 Nishio as Chief Cabinet Secretary associated himself with a memorandum to the American government in Washington suggesting that Japan's security after independence could only be safeguarded by a Japanese defence build-up and a security treaty with the United States.[16]

Since the issue of neutralism divided the factions so bitterly after the outbreak of the Korean war seven months later, it seems a little surprising that the policy should have been adopted without a fight in 1949. We have seen that at least some members of the Nishio and Suzuki factions had formulated their contrasting attitudes to the question before this date, but the issue was hardly yet important to them and the party was still preoccupied with domestic issues and factional rivalry at the expense of foreign affairs.

Having established that the neutralist policies of the JSP originated with the Suzuki faction, it remains to relate these policies to the faction's experiences and ideology. Three important factors seem to have been involved:

First, the faction shared in full measure the mood of pacifism which pervaded Japan for several years after 1945. Support for the 'pacifist clause' of the 1946 Constitution (implying for many, a nation strictly and literally unarmed) extended well beyond the ranks of socialists and 'progressive' intellectuals for whom indeed it had become a deeply genuine article of faith. The

Suzuki faction, having fallen foul of the militarists in pre-war days, was second to none in this regard.

Second, any form of dependence on capitalist powers was rejected for ideological reasons. 'The defeat of capitalism', said Sakisaka Itsurō, a leading *Rōnō-ha* intellectual, 'would remove the main causes of war. If the whole world became socialist . . . the cause of today's wars would disappear.'[17]

Third, dependence on the communist powers was rejected on grounds that at first sight may seem less straightforward. Few in Japan saw the new régime in China as a military threat, and left wing socialists could welcome the new leaders there as fellow socialists in a country which had close cultural and historical ties with Japan. The Soviet Union was also regarded by them with more admiration than apprehension. Despite these affinities, however, a self-consciously 'neutralist' line was chosen, emphasizing Japan's independence from the communists as well as from the capitalists. It is interesting that Suzuki, in his defence of neutralism, argued that Japan need not fear China since the Chinese would need Japanese help in the development of their country.[18] The implication was that Japan, as a nation of stature in the Far East, would be able to assert her independence without the need for entangling military alliances with capitalist powers against communist neighbours.

There was an important connection here with ideological tradition. The Suzuki faction was on the closest of terms with a group of intellectuals who still professed the *Rōnō-ha* view of revolutionary strategy. The essence of the *Rōnō-ha* doctrine was that Japan was at a level of 'advanced' capitalism and therefore ready for a proletarian 'one-stage' revolution. This, as we have already indicated, predisposed the faction to take a recognizably nationalist view of foreign affairs : Japan, as an advanced nation, should assert her national independence, for the international cause of peace and socialism.

It may be concluded that the neutralist policy introduced into the JSP in 1949 was the result of two types of motivation : on the one hand, a desire to immunize Japan against the possibility of involvement in another war; on the other, a belief that she could reasonably hope to be able to stand aloof and unharmed from international feuds. The first was already present in socialist thinking in 1946 (and led to a rejection of any kind of neutrality at that period). The second sprang from fear of Japan's becoming an American satellite in the cold war, and was fed by the 'national Marxism' of the now dominant Suzuki faction.

4

THE GREAT SPLIT

Despite initial indications of a united approach to foreign policy, the hectic tide of events in 1950 and 1951 brought forward issues which split the party wide open. The momentous importance for Japan's future of her national security and choice of allies scarcely needs stressing. For the socialists, moreover, this was a matter which brought to the surface in their most sensitive form latent ideological differences of basic importance. Was Japan to continue her close association with the United States, or proclaim neutrality with her independence? Was she to remain unarmed, as the 1946 Constitution had made her, or to rearm under American auspices, as the Americans were beginning to urge? Should she accept a peace treaty which the Soviet Union, China and certain other countries refused to sign, or should she postpone independence until a 'total' peace treaty could be concluded?

All these questions exacerbated the tensions between Marxist and Fabian, pre-war pro-militarist and pre-war anti-militarist, members of one personal faction and members of another, until a split could no longer be avoided. Underlying these events was a continuing overall trend to the left within the party.

The outbreak of the Korean war—a mere six months after the JSP had adopted a foreign policy of neutrality—put the party in a dilemma. Its support for the UN, which had taken prompt action against the North Korean forces, was not easily squared with the idea of a neutralist Japan. The party's first official reaction was expressed in a Central Executive Committee resolution dated 5 July 1950.

On the cause of the war the resolution was uncompromising: 'The immediate cause of the Korean war was the resort to force

39

by the People's Republic of North Korea in an attempt to unify Korea. This must be seen in some sense as an aggressive development of communist revolution.'[1] It went on to express support, though in general terms, for UN action. It held, however, that Japan under Occupation control had no obligation to support the UN in Korea beyond what SCAP required of her, and therefore urged *de facto* neutrality. It reiterated the JSP argument that a peace treaty should be concluded with all the belligerents, while admitting that with the outbreak of the Korean war the prospects for such a treaty had 'somewhat receded'.

Shortly afterwards, a national newspaper addressed a questionnaire to the party about its attitudes to a peace settlement and to security. The official reply admitted that Japan's security depended to some extent on the UN action in Korea, but contended that a proper attitude for Japan should be 'moral condemnation' of North Korean aggression, combined with non-interference in the actual struggle. The UN should guarantee the security of Japan, but Japan was not in a position (because of the pacifist clause of the Constitution) to co-operate in any positive fashion.[2]

In the trade union movement, as in the JSP, comparatively little public mention had been made of foreign policy until the outbreak of the Korean war. The beginning of hostilities only shortly preceded the inauguration of a new national trade union federation, *Sōhyō*.[3] This federation came about as part of an internal reaction against communist attempts to control the trade union movement, and its birth was probably facilitated by the Economic and Scientific Section of SCAP. It was, however, far from homogeneous and contained much the same factional elements as the JSP. The inaugural Congress of *Sōhyō* in July 1950 issued a statement on the Korean war similar in content to that of the JSP. The war was blamed on North Korean aggression, moral support was expressed for the UN force, but for practical purposes Japanese neutralism was enjoined. An appendix to the statement called for a peace treaty between Japan and all nations which had fought against her in World War II.[4]

A further issue which caused difficulty in both the JSP and

Sōhyō was rearmament. On the outbreak of war in Korea, General MacArthur authorized the formation of a 'Police Reserve' of 75,000 men and an increase of 8,000 in the size of the existing Maritime Safety Force. This move was prompted by a wave of violence attributed to communists (the Cominform had criticized the Communist Party in January 1950 for its previous moderation) and by the withdrawal of most of the American troops in Japan for service in Korea.

Although the Police Reserve was only designed to maintain internal order and was clearly inadequate to defend Japan against external aggression, its creation set off a nationwide discussion of the merits of rearmament. The question sharply divided the left and right wings of the JSP, but they first attempted to find a compromise formula. The party made an initial statement on 18 July supporting the establishment of the Police Reserve provided that its purpose was to combat domestic subversion only.[5] Conditions were, however, attached: it was to be formed 'in a democratic manner' and was not to be given a militaristic training such as might further the reactionary ends of the government. Its equipment was to be strictly limited, since a heavily armed force would impose an intolerable strain on the economy, and so on the people's standard of living.

This statement did not satisfy the left wing and the intra-party dispute came to a head at the JSP Congress of January 1951. This Congress took place shortly after the Chinese intervention in the Korean war, and at a time of extreme international tension in which Japanese rearmament had become a pressing issue. In his New Year message to the Japanese people on 1 January 1951 General MacArthur suggested that the Japanese might, in view of the international situation, consider some measure of rearmament.[6]

In an atmosphere of intense national debate, the right wing Nishio faction presented a resolution to the January Congress calling for the acceptance if necessary of a 'partial' peace treaty, rejecting neutralism and supporting membership of the western camp as the bastion of freedom, and asserting the right of self-defence against communist aggression.[7]

This uncompromising call to join the western camp was rejected by the Congress by 342 votes to 81, and a left wing resolution, sponsored by the Suzuki faction, endorsed the 'three peace principles'.[8] Another successful resolution sponsored by the left attacked the idea of rearmament;[9] its substance was that Japanese rearmament would be geared to the defence, not of Japan, but of American interests in the cold war. This was an affront to Japan, and could involve her in a third world war. Moreover, it would be economically burdensome, politically and socially dangerous and militarily unnecessary, besides provoking Japan's neighbours and reducing the chances of a peace treaty with all the former belligerents. On a wave of pacifist sentiment, the resolution carried the day, and a fourth 'peace principle'— 'opposition to rearmament'—was added to the previous three.

The second Congress of *Sōhyō*, held in March 1951, endorsed a policy close to the left wing position at the JSP Congress in January. The *Sōhyō* Congress did not issue any statement on the Korean war, but included the four peace principles in its 'Action Platform'.[10] Its resolutions were now in striking contrast to those of the previous year, as was its attitude to membership of the International Confederation of Free Trade Unions (ICFTU). Whereas the 1950 Congress had determined that *Sōhyō* should seek membership of ICFTU,[11] in 1951 a further resolution to this effect was defeated. ICFTU had been set up in 1949 in opposition to the communist-dominated World Federation of Trade Unions (WFTU). Thus by 1951 *Sōhyō* had clearly swung left.

In part this was because in December 1950 it had been joined by the left wing federation *Shinsambetsu*, which served to increase the number of neutralists at the 1951 Congress.[12] More important, however, was the isolation of the *Sōhyō* right wing. Shortly before the accession of *Shinsambetsu* there was a serious split in *Sōdōmei*, the most important trade union federation affiliated with *Sōhyō*. The left wing faction of *Sōdōmei*, under its brilliant but erratic leader Takano Minoru, wished the federation to dissolve and the individual trade unions of which it was formed to affiliate only with *Sōhyō*. The right wing faction wished it to continue independently within *Sōhyō*. *Sōdōmei* thus became the exclusive preserve of the right wing faction based principally on the textile workers' and seamen's unions, which were also the basis of support for the Nishio faction of the JSP.[13]

Thus by early 1951 the right wings of both *Sōhyō* and the JSP were at loggerheads with the left and in a minority. At the March 1951 Congress of *Sōhyō* the combined forces of the Takano faction and *Shinsambetsu* ensured the passage of left wing policy resolutions. In any case the left had been gaining ground in the party and trade unions alike since the fall of the coalition government and the disastrous 1949 election. Within the ranks of the left, however, there were important divisions of opinion about foreign affairs. *Shinsambetsu,* inspired by its ex-communist leader Hosoya Matsuta, advocated a 'third force' neutralism and opposed affiliation with ICFTU because it was part of the 'free world'.[14] Takano, on the other hand, apparently wanted Japan to be neutralist, but still looked with favour on the 'free world'—at least its 'progressive elements'—and thought *Sōhyō* should affiliate with ICFTU.[15] The surprising thing about Takano is that within three years he had reversed his position and was calling on Japan to back the 'forces of peace', by which he meant the communist camp.

Since this later policy was one which, once formulated, he never again abandoned, his earlier and very different position is in its way something of a mystery.

There is good reason to suppose that the support given by SCAP to the formation of an anti-communist trade union federation was used by Takano for his own purposes. According to this hypothesis, he wished to gain control of the new federation and to triumph over his rivals within the trade union movement. He had achieved the first of these aims when he was elected Secretary-General of *Sōhyō* at its second Congress in 1951, a post which he retained until 1954. Up to 1950 the most dangerous of his rivals were communists, but by the end of the Occupation in 1952 they were a negligible force in the labour movement, having become subject to the purge regulations in 1950 after the JCP, on Cominform orders, had turned to militant anti-Americanism. In that year the Japanese government, with the approval of SCAP, banned the communist-dominated federation of trade unions known as *Zenrōren* (Zenkoku Rōdō Kumiai Renraku Kyōgikai) (National Liaison Council of Trade

Unions), which was already gravely weakened. This ban removed the last significant competitor of the emergent *Sōhyō*, whose leaders were roundly criticized by *Shinsambetsu* for making a minimum of protest at the purge of communist unionists.[16]

Two or three years later, however, Takano was to make the quip that in incubating *Sōhyō*, SCAP had 'hatched a chicken which turned out to be an ugly duckling'.

In the JSP between January and September 1951 the contrasting attitudes of left and right altered little. The centre, however, was much strengthened by the lifting from its leaders of the purge regulations which had kept them out of all political activities since early in the Occupation. Kawakami Jōtarō, a Christian and veteran socialist, had been purged because of his official position during the war in the Imperial Rule Assistance Association. The Kawakami faction, which embraced most of this centre group, was now placed in a stronger position to fulfil its traditional role as mediator between right and left. As befitted such a role, the views expressed by the faction on the peace settlement partook of the arguments of both sides. On the one hand it inclined towards the Nishio faction's support for a 'partial' peace treaty as the lesser evil in the circumstances, but on the other it stood with the Suzuki faction in opposing the proposed Security Treaty. On rearmament it held that such a step should not in principle be dismissed, but that a decision should be postponed.[17]

By mid-1951 a complete split in the party began to appear inevitable, and the eventual allegiance of Kawakami's centre faction became a matter of crucial importance to all. In the end it proved possible for the centre and right to adjust their views, which substantially differed only on the Security Treaty. They devised a compromise, namely that both factions should publicly support the Treaty, with the proviso that after independence foreign troops should be rapidly withdrawn.[18]

The anticipated split took place at a stormy party Congress held shortly after the Peace Treaty and Security Treaty were signed at San Francisco in September 1951. Japanese socialism was now for more than four years to be represented by two quite evenly matched parties, each claiming the title 'Japan Socialist Party'.

Since the attitudes taken by the factions at this crucial Congress are of such importance, they may be conveniently summarized at this point.[19]

The Nishio and Suzuki factions differed fundamentally about Japan's overall international position.

The right wing Nishio faction rejected neutralism and accepted the principle of alliance with the 'free world'. It argued that neutralism, to be effective, required the consent of the great powers. This was unlikely to be given, since communist ideology did not respect neutrality in others, and Japan's geographical position and industrial potential made her a prize even more tempting in that she was unarmed. Neutralism was also incompatible with the duty of furnishing sanctions if ordered to do so by the UN.

The left wing Suzuki faction, on the contrary, accepted neutralism and rejected alliance with the 'free world'. It maintained that alliance with the west was likely to provoke communist aggression and to make it more difficult to solve Asian conflicts, including the Korean war. Such an alliance might involve Japan in the duty of participating in these struggles, and thus in a world war also. Since alliance with the west meant subservience to the United States and probably the resurgence of militarism in Japan, it would be a threat to other Asian countries (particularly China) which had suffered at Japanese hands. Therefore a third road should be taken, neither capitalist nor communist, but that of social democracy and emergent Asian nationalism.

The application of these arguments to the problem of the Peace Treaty gave divergent results. The Nishio faction held that the opportunity should be taken to conclude a peace treaty, even if certain nations that had fought against Japan did not sign it. (The alternative would mean indefinite postponement of independence.) It denied that an 'incomplete' peace treaty would revive militarism, or that it was a threat to China. The Suzuki faction believed that it was an illusion to support an 'incomplete' peace treaty merely on the grounds that it would bring independence. Such a settlement would limit Japanese sovereignty (especially since foreign troops were to be stationed for an indefinite period) and threaten her economic and political independence. The two factions also argued concerning the Security Treaty and rearmament. According to the Nishio faction, an independent Japan had the right to defend herself militarily, but this should be limited to the defence of Japanese territory. Although eventually her forces would be adequate for the task, in the short run she would need what was termed 'collective security', which she could obtain in accordance with the United Nations Charter. This meant the stationing of American troops, preferably, but not necessarily, in the capacity of UN forces.[20]

The Suzuki faction held that the decision on defence should be left until after an 'overall' peace treaty had been signed, and then be decided by the 'free will of the people' on the basis of the 'pacifist clause' of the Constitution. Until such a peace treaty, Japan's security should be guaranteed by treaties of non-aggression with her neighbours. In this way it should be possible to secure the abolition of the Sino-Soviet Treaty (the Thirty Year Treaty of Friendship, Alliance and Mutual Assistance of 14 February 1950) which specifically cited Japan as a potential aggressor. The ideal of security (which need not in its opinion be remote) was universal 'collective security' by the UN.

In between these positions the Kawakami faction advanced arguments similar to those of the Nishio faction except on the question of the Security Treaty, to which it objected on the grounds that the stationing of foreign troops was a limitation of sovereignty and national independence.

Thus while most members of the Nishio faction supported both Treaties and the Suzuki faction opposed both Treaties, the Kawakami faction supported the Peace Treaty and opposed the Security Treaty.

Of the conclusions which may be drawn from this account of the development of socialist attitudes to foreign and defence policy in 1950–1, perhaps the most important is the great significance which came to be attached to the question of rearmament. It was this problem rather than any other which dominated discussions at the January 1951 Congress, and the enunciation of a fourth 'peace principle'—opposition to rearmament— was a major achievement for the Suzuki faction.

This controversy touched on a basic ideological difference between the left and right wings of the party. Essentially the Suzuki faction believed that domestic and international conflict could be resolved into a struggle between socialism and capitalism, while the Nishio faction maintained that the struggle fundamental to the contemporary world was that between democracy and communism. Thus in the famous Morito-Inamura ideological dispute in the JSP in 1949,[21] Inamura Junzō, for the left, had argued that the party should be composed of the working class alone, that only the working class, as a disciplined force, was capable of carrying out a revolution, and that in order to conduct a revolution it was necessary to fight capitalism on all fronts with the same ruthlessness as could be expected from it. The argument rested on the premise that capitalism would not easily surrender, but would take any opportunity of reasserting the dictatorial position which it had lost with Japan's defeat. Armed forces, as a potential weapon for the oppression of the working class, should therefore not in any circumstances be put in the hands of the capitalists.[22] Morito Tatsuo, for the right, had argued that socialism should be achieved gradually, by parliamentary means, and the JSP should be a 'people's party', not the exclusive preserve of the working class in a narrow sense. This was a view which found communism its worst enemy, and thus it is not difficult to explain why the Nishio faction should have been willing to accept some measure of rearmament as a deterrent against communism.

It is interesting to compare the attitudes of the factions to rearmament and security in 1951 with their pre-war record in relation to militarism. The Nishio faction, because of its consistent support for parliamentary democracy and its opposition to extremism, had shown some resistance to the excesses of the militarists in the late 1930s. By the 1950s, however, it was more concerned with the communist threat than with a revival of militarism. The Suzuki faction, which had the cleanest pre-war anti-militarist record of any group (with the exception of the communists) now made much of the danger of putting arms into the hands of those who had previously misused them. The Kawakami faction, having been temporarily weakened by SCAP's purge of its leaders, was more reticent and equivocal.

This was probably indicative of a desire not to draw attention to its pre-war near-fascist record, although in its attitude to the Security Treaty in 1951 may perhaps be detected a hint of its past militant nationalism.

The JSP continued to drift to the left during 1950 and 1951. The Suzuki faction profited from the discredit brought upon the Nishio faction for participating in the coalition governments of 1947–8; Left Socialists also gained ground electorally and in the trade unions by the sudden loss of support for the communists following the Cominform criticism of the JCP in January 1950, by a generalized reaction against the United States in the last years of the Occupation, and by the wave of pacifism following the outbreak of the Korean war. Paradoxically, as we have seen, SCAP also played its part in consolidating the non-communist left wing factions in the trade unions. The relationship between the leadership of the trade union movement and that of the JSP was, as always, extremely close. The right wing of *Sōdōmei*, for instance, had the very closest ties with the Nishio faction of the JSP. Certain rivalries, however, such as that between *Shinsambetsu* and the Takano faction, did not have their counterpart in the JSP, and Takano's peculiar relationship with SCAP was something whose immediate influence was confined to *Sōhyō*. It is scarcely possible to conclude that the growing neutralist atmosphere in the JSP and the trade unions was something which entered the JSP by way of the trade unions, or vice versa. Both organizations, in their own roughly parallel ways, were influenced by the same events and issues. In both, the questions of independence, security and rearmament served to divide right from left, and increasingly to isolate the right. Thus in both, although the timing was somewhat different, a right-left split could not be avoided.

5

NEUTRALISM AND 'SOCIAL DEMOCRACY'

The Left Socialist Party (LSP) which emerged from the 'great split' of October 1951 had, as was to be expected, a foreign policy of neutralism. In the period up to the beginning of serious negotiations with the Right Socialists in 1954, this policy became markedly more anti-American and anti-European. The party, however, resisted pressures emanating from the trade unions for it to become openly pro-communist.

While the anti-western bias which 'neutralism' came to assume has to be explained mainly in terms of circumstances external to the party, it was the situation within the party that stemmed this initial drift after it had reached a certain point. Two factors were at work. The tradition of the *Rōnō-ha*, which most of the LSP leaders inherited, divided them ideologically (despite some similarity in their ultimate aims) from the communists. But it was also crucial that the main factions in fact succeeded in dividing the principal party offices more or less harmoniously among themselves, and could thus present a united front against an ideological challenge.

The first few months after the split were ones of adjustment to a new and unfamiliar Japan that had gained her independence but was still closely linked to America through a bilateral security pact. To meet this situation the LSP formulated a policy, owing much to the Indian example, which it called 'third force neutralism'. The Action Policy adopted by the LSP Congress of January 1952 defined the policy in the following terms:

> What is called a 'third force' consists of all those forces working to prevent World War III. Such forces do exist in America and the Soviet Union, but it is rather the world outside these two countries that contains the third force.[1]

The Action Policy went on to designate three main constituent elements: socialist movements in advanced capitalist countries (mostly belonging to the Socialist International), countries newly independent since World War II (in particular India, Burma, Indonesia and parts of the Arab world) and 'genuine democrats in any area'.

Significant examples of 'third force' action in the interests of world peace included the British Labour government's efforts to restrain the Americans from using nuclear weapons after Chinese entry into the Korean war; the dismissal of General MacArthur; left wing opposition to rearmament in West Germany and Japan and world-wide opposition to the Japanese peace settlement; and attempts by minor powers at the UN to convene a disarmament conference.

The main strength of the 'third force' was said to lie in the first of the three groups, namely socialist movements in advanced capitalist countries. These, unlike the Soviet Union, were democratic and, unlike the United States, were socialist. The newly independent countries were put firmly in second place, although their strong sense of national independence was applauded and their ruling classes were praised as 'not ultra-reactionary'. At least one commentator noted that this emphasis, and especially the importance attached to the Socialist International, contrasted with previous Left Socialist attitudes.[2] For instance, their representatives at the Frankfurt Conference of the International in June-July 1951 had clashed with other delegates on the questions of defence and neutrality.[3]

European socialism was, moreover, the lynch-pin of the 'third force' argument only for a short period. The Left Socialist Action Policy for 1953 stressed rather the newly-independent Asian states and in particular socialist movements within those states. The European-dominated Socialist International came once more under fire from party leaders.[4] This change was undoubtedly connected with the first plenary session of the Asian Socialist Conference (ASC) in Rangoon in January 1953, shortly before the Left Socialist Congress of that year.

Although the idea of an organization of Asian socialists was first discussed as early as 1947, no concrete steps were taken until March 1952, when a Preliminary Meeting was held between representatives of the socialist parties of India, Burma and Indonesia, with representatives of Japanese socialism attending as observers. Here the Japanese Left Socialists (but not the Right Socialists) supported the Indian delegate Lohia in his campaign for a primarily Asian 'third force' not tied to European socialism.[5]

A much larger number of delegations were invited to the first plenary session in January 1953. The most controversial issues were relations with the Socialist International, and neutralism. On the first the LSP delegates clashed with Clement Attlee, who was there as the representative of the Socialist International, maintaining that the Socialist International was divorced from Asian aspirations, especially on questions of defence.[6]

Such was the diversity of views on neutralism that it proved impossible to formulate a universally acceptable resolution in which 'third force' and 'neutralism' should be key concepts.[7] The body which emerged from the first plenary session of the ASC was closer to the Socialist International in stated aims and organization than had been envisaged by most of the participants at the Preliminary Meeting. Nevertheless, the LSP seems to have regarded the session as a qualified victory for its point of view.[8]

An alliance between Japanese socialism and the developing and newly independent nations of southern Asia appealed to the Left Socialists for a number of reasons: for one thing 'socialist planning' was in vogue in some of the countries of the area. Indeed, the achievements of planning in mainland China sometimes led to a tentative inclusion of China within the sphere of the 'third force'.[9] Again, the support which most of the European socialist parties gave to NATO made them less comfortable allies than socialist-inclined groups in uncommitted countries such as India. Finally, the anti-colonialism prevalent in southern Asia had something in common with the anti-imperialism of the LSP. Japan, after all, had only recently regained her freedom from the alien rule of the Allied Occupation.

With independence, moreover, her ties with the United States appeared to have been consolidated rather than relaxed. The form of the 1951 Security Treaty and accompanying Administrative Agreement (which governed the terms under which

WAYNESBURG COLLEGE LIBRARY
WAYNESBURG, PA.

American forces were to be stationed in Japan) were taken by the left as evidence of a lack of genuine independence. In particular, the Security Treaty had neither a specific time limit nor provisions for consultation between the signatories (except in cases of domestic disturbances). American forces stationed in Japan could apparently be used in operations in other parts of the Far East. Article XXV of the Administrative Agreement provided that Japan had to give the American forces free facilities and a 'defence contribution of $155 million per annum'. Article XVII, which seemed reminiscent of western powers' extraterritorial privileges of the late nineteenth century, exempted American servicemen stationed in Japan from the jurisdiction of the Japanese courts.

Public opinion polls indicate that opposition to American military bases in Japan increased between 1950 and 1953 (and it was to grow even greater).[10] This swing of opinion, if genuine, presents us with the apparent paradox that the American military presence in independent Japan caused wider resentment than had the existence of an American force of Occupation.

The change in public mood was paralleled by an intensification of anti-Americanism on the part of the LSP between its Congresses of 1952 and 1953. The resolutions passed by the 1952 Congress referred to American world policies in only mildly critical terms and avoided the term 'American imperialism'.[11] The party's Action Policy for 1953, however, spoke of a dangerous reactionary trend in United States foreign policy under the new Eisenhower Administration, and designated Japan a 'political dependency' and 'military colony' of the United States. The tone of the document was much more critical of America than that of the previous year. Nevertheless, it vigorously restated the principles of the 'third force' and rejected alignment with the Soviet Union or communist China, including participation in the pro-communist peace movement.[12]

The wording of the 1953 Action Policy reflected a mounting storm of ideological dispute which was to preoccupy most members of the party for some time to come. It is to the nature of this dispute that we must now turn.

On the one hand most members of the party executive had long-standing associations with the *Rōnō-ha* tradition, having been in many cases participants in its political and ideological battles since the 1920s. They were now strongly backed by an intellectual pressure group on the fringes of the party, known as the *Shakaishugi Kyōkai* (Socialist Association). This group was still dominated by the original founder of the *Rōnō-ha*, the ageing Yamakawa Hitoshi. Yamakawa's central and oft-repeated theme was that Japanese 'monopoly capital' had achieved a sufficient degree of strength in the economy for a proletarian-socialist revolution to be able to succeed without the intervening 'bourgeois-democratic' revolution.

The JCP, on the other hand, was heir to the *Kōza-ha* doctrine of a two-stage revolution. Communists now spoke of a revolution of 'national liberation' which must precede any attempt to establish true socialism. 'National liberation' however, was something much easier to understand while Japan had a security agreement and other close ties with the United States, than it would have been during the 1920s when Japan herself controlled a number of colonies. They maintained that the pre-war domination of Japan by 'feudal elements' had been modified by the experience during the Occupation of 'international monopoly capital', whose stranglehold over the economy must be broken as the first essential step of revolution.[13]

As we have seen, the LSP Action Policy for 1953 used trenchant language about the United States. Nevertheless, it took pains to differentiate the terms 'political dependency' and 'military colony', which it used itself to define Japan's relationship with America, from the formulation preferred by the JCP—'a true colony'.[14] Lest this distinction appear over-subtle, it is as well to remember the ideological undertones which it evoked.

In foreign policy, moreover, the implications were important. If, as it seemed to most LSP leaders, Japan by virtue of her industrial strength enjoyed at any rate a degree of national independence, it followed in their thinking that in her struggle against American influence she should stop well short of alliance with countries of the communist bloc, and the party should refrain from joining communist-dominated organizations. Doctrines of neutralism and 'third force' were thus easily acceptable. However, those (such as the JCP leadership) who believed 'national liberation' was the necessary first stage of revolution, were prepared to welcome allies from the communist countries since those were the most powerful and obvious allies to be found.

Up to 1953 this controversy had served to distinguish the JCP and LSP, with each positioned firmly on opposite sides of the fence. Now, however, the intensified anti-American feeling which had manifested itself on the left as a whole came to be reflected in divisions within the LSP itself. The immediate cause of these divisions was a parallel series of developments in the trade union movement, which now for a time takes the centre of the stage. It is on events in the trade unions that we must now focus our attention before returning to examine their repercussions in the LSP.

Sōhyō, under the leadership of Takano Minoru, had already moved a considerable distance to the left since its debut in 1950 as a supposedly anti-communist federation of labour. In 1952 it engaged in some particularly bitter strikes against new labour legislation, and at its annual Congress carried a resolution to support only the Left Socialists in the coming general election.[15] It also endorsed the LSP policy of 'third force' neutralism. These policies were, however, opposed from within the federation by the textile workers' and seamen's unions. By 1953 their combined organization, *Minrōren* (Democratic Labour League), was openly at war with a group composed of most of the left wing leadership, in the interests of more moderate policies.

At *Sōhyō's* Congress of July 1953 it became clear that Takano was determined to pull the movement still further to the left. Before the full Congress began the draft Action Policy was long fought over in committee, where three main points of contention were revealed.

The first and most important was Takano's so-called 'peace forces' argument, the exact nature of which was left obscure in the Action Policy and not clearly elucidated by Takano in his exposition of that Policy to the Congress itself.[16] He did not, for instance, specifically identify any particular countries with the 'peace forces' which he thought *Sōhyō* should back, but his criticism of the United States and favourable references to both the Soviet Union and communist China indicated clearly enough the direction of his thinking. Moreover the Action Policy omitted any reference to 'third force' neutralism such as the previous Congress had endorsed. Takano explained this omission with the argument that merely to support the 'third force' would unduly restrict the socialist movement in its struggle for peace.[17]

The second related point was whether *Sōhyō* should seek affiliation with the anti-communist ICFTU. In the end, no change was made from the previous year's policy that *Sōhyō* should remain outside the world body, though individual unions were free to join if they wished.

On the third controversial issue, however, a decision was made in favour of change, namely to seek friendly relations with the All-China Federation of Trade Unions in Peking.[18]

Why was this ambiguously expressed, yet transparently pro-communist policy platform introduced into *Sōhyō* at this juncture? One reason seems to lie in the current world situation, for Stalin had died some months previously and his death was followed by a Soviet peace offensive with widespread international repercussions. Takano made clear that he regarded this as a major initiative in the interests of world peace, and considered the settlement of the Korean war as one of its achievements.[19]

In contrast, recent American foreign policies gave Japanese socialists little grounds for optimism. They were quick to detect in the new Eisenhower Administration a more inflexible approach to world problems than had been evinced by its predecessor.[20] It was, after all, in June 1953 that the United States opened negotiations for the application of American Mutual Security Assistance to Japan. The condition of such assistance—that Japan should build her own defence forces capable of dealing with external aggression—naturally convinced most socialists that their country was about to be turned into an armed bastion against communism, whereby she might well become embroiled in a war that was none of her own making.[21]

The most important reason, however, must lie in the motives and personality of Takano himself. Takano's role is puzzling in two ways. First, it would appear that he changed his view with remarkable suddenness. The question of the 'peace forces' apparently did not arise at all until after the general elections of April, up to which time Takano and his supporters continued to give their blessing to the 'third force' neutralism of the LSP. He was, for instance, one of the Left Socialist delegates to the ASC in January. Second, Takano's close association since the 1920s with the *Rōnō-ha* stream of socialist thought indicates a sudden jump into ideological heresy, since the 'peace forces' argument had about it the stamp of the rival *Kōza-ha* tradition. On closer inspection, however, these two factors do not seem quite so surprising. Takano's earlier views of the 'third force' seem to have been distinctly idiosyncratic, and there is evidence that his radical change of position was already in the making about a year before he actually announced it.[22] The importance of Takano's ties with the *Rōnō-ha* may also have been less binding than it would be natural to suppose. Evidence from interviews conducted by the writer suggests that during the 1930s he may have had significant contacts with the banned communist party, and that the influences upon him were rather more radical than was the case with most of the *Rōnō-ha* supporters.[23]

Whatever his individual motives in taking the left wing course which he decided upon in 1953, his action had a profound effect not only upon *Sōhyō* (where it precipitated immediate secession on the part of certain right wing unions and open criticism from moderates) but also in the LSP.

The LSP's first official reaction was to claim that there was no real difference between the 'third force' and the 'peace forces'.[24] This statement, however, merely served to conceal a very real division within the party which had already manifested itself in the discussions of a committee set up the previous January to draw up a new party platform.[25] In November, after lengthy discussions, a majority draft was announced together with a minority draft prepared by the sole *Sōhyō* representative on the committee.[26]

The majority draft bore all the marks of the *Rōnō-ha* tradition. The main 'enemy' was domestic monopoly capital whose ties with American capital were only of secondary importance. The struggle against American financial control was not to be ignored, but at the same time it should not be allowed to develop into what the JCP liked to call a 'movement for national liberation'. Neutralism was to be used as a weapon both against

American 'imperialism' and against 'control by Japanese mono-poly finance capital'.[27]

The dissenting draft, in contrast, made the usual *Kōza-ha* points that Japan was under the complete control of American 'imperialism', and that therefore absolute priority should be given to a 'national struggle against imperialist control'.

With publication of these drafts, the party executive decided to throw the weight of its authority against the dissidents, whose numbers, though small, were obviously sufficient to have a disruptive effect. It issued a directive forbidding members of the party from participating in joint struggles with the JCP, and insisting on adherence to 'third force' neutralism as the basis of the party's foreign policy.[28] Such a show of firmness called down the wrath of Takano on the heads of the party's leaders and at one stage tension reached the pitch where rumours that the dissidents would form a new party had to be officially denied. Indeed Takano led his followers out of the *Shakaishugi Kyōkai* —fountainhead of the party's main stream ideology—to which most leading members of both the LSP and *Sōhyō* belonged.[29] The party's Youth Group, always a hotbed of radicalism, also split in the same fashion.[30]

Despite the acute embarrassment which this movement caused the party executive, Takano in fact had little hope of carrying off a substantial section of the party to form a new party of his own. Even within *Sōhyō* his position was becoming precarious, as shown by the fact that a year later he was ousted from the leadership by a more moderate man, Ōta Kaoru. His support in the LSP itself was concentrated in the small Matsumoto faction. This faction, which later took the appellation *Heiwa Dōshikai* (Association of Friends of Peace) was to remain over a long period ideologically distinct in important respects from the rest of the party. It was never, however, a serious contender for party leadership.

In 1953 the success of the party leaders in meeting Takano's challenge was partly due, as we have already seen, to the strength of the *Rōnō-ha* ideology and its tradition among the Left Socialists. Another reason was undoubtedly the discrediting of the JCP because of its violent tactics after responding to the

Cominform criticism of 1950, and the corresponding flight of votes to the LSP.

A further important factor was the factional situation within the LSP. The party consisted of four factions—all subdivisions of the left wing grouping before the 1951 split. Two of these (Suzuki and Wada) between them accounted for most of the party's Diet members, and two (Nomizo and Matsumoto) had each only a handful of adherents and were influential only to the extent that they could influence the main factions. Over the period the leaders of three of the factions (Suzuki, Nomizo and Wada) occupied respectively the Chairmanship, the Secretary-Generalship and the Chairmanship of the Policy Committee, in other words the most important positions in the party. Commentators noted that Suzuki had support not only from his own 'main-stream' faction but also from those led by Wada and Nomizo, and that these three factions were able to work, at least during 1952 and 1953, in substantial harmony.[31] It seems that the ability of the party to work out a mutually advantageous division of the key party posts lessened the disruptive nature of ideological quarrels. Had this not been so, a particular faction might well have been tempted to turn ideological divisions to its own factional advantage.

In conclusion it is perhaps as well to summarize the development of a Left Socialist foreign policy between October 1951 and January 1954. 'Third force' neutralism—a policy initially formulated before the 1951 split—gradually took on an Asian rather than European colouring, and its anti-American content became steadily more marked. A similar trend in *Sōhyō* went further, and from mid-1953 the *Sōhyō* leadership adopted a pro-communist position. This subjected the LSP to division and strain, but the party remained intact and stuck in essence to its original foreign policy.

These events can be explained by a variety of factors, political, ideological and factional. The 'Asian' tone of the 1953 Action Policy was affected by the ASC whose aspirations seemed to the party most nearly to coincide with its own emergent 'anti-imperialism'. Hostility to the United States was accentuated by the continued American presence in independent Japan and by general trends in American foreign policy. The 'peace forces' argument in *Sōhyō* was connected with Takano's response to the Soviet peace offensive, his reaction against the United States, and perhaps most importantly, his own character and ideological background. When the socialist movement split in 1951 the LSP was suddenly placed in the position of being able freely to stress its differences from the Right Socialists. At the same time a tradition of ideology served to distinguish the party's general attitudes from those of the communists and pro-communists on its left flank. For this reason, and because internal factional relations were not allowed to get out of hand, the pro-communist foreign policy presented by *Sōhyō* did not make much headway in the party, and 'third force' neutralism was strongly reasserted.

Nevertheless, a truly neutralist approach to world affairs was to prove difficult to uphold in the face of pressures that were soon to beset the party.

6

NEUTRALISM AND
'DEMOCRATIC SOCIALISM'

We have observed how the Left Socialist Party, although it had to meet a serious challenge to its 'third force' neutralism from the extreme left, emerged from the struggle with the policy intact and its leading factions still largely united.

The Right Socialists, in their own way, sought to present what they called 'democratic socialism' as a third road in world affairs, although they rejected the idea of neutralism between the communists and the west. For the first two years of its existence the Right Socialist Party (RSP) appeared to be united about this policy, but towards the end of 1953 its official views on defence and security met a serious challenge from its own right wing. This precipitated a major rift.

What this policy really implied, and why the RSP failed—even more signally than the LSP over *its* policy—to remain of one mind, is the subject of this chapter.

Soon after its formation the party took a critical look at the 'third force' neutralism of its Left Socialist counterparts. The Left, it argued in a policy statement,[1] had failed to appreciate the difference between an ideological 'middle road' and a neutralist bloc opting out of all defensive alliances. European socialism and Asian nationalism were indeed potential forces for peace in the world. The new nations of Asia had a healthy determination to be independent, both from their former colonial masters and from communism. Yet in the RSP view the necessity for collective security against aggression remained, especially, indeed, for an unarmed Japan. European socialist parties were, after all, well aware of this fact, and had rejected a neutralist solution.

On the positive side, the Right Socialists gave their whole-hearted support to the Socialist International, a body which was anti-communist, in favour of collective security and the international embodiment of 'democratic socialism'.

'Democratic socialism' may be called the party's 'ideology', although it was quite distinct from the semi-Marxist 'social democracy' of the LSP. It is therefore important to see what Right Socialists meant by it. The essential content could be set out as follows: Reject communism for its doctrines of violent revolution and dictatorship of the proletariat, but oppose conservatism for its intention of preserving the capitalist structure of society. Socialism must be achieved democratically. This means government by parliamentary majority and implementation of socialism by consent. Allow opposition parties to function freely and bow to the verdict of the electorate if it is adverse. Political revolution must be gradual, but the snare of reformist capitalism must be avoided. Socialism means socialization of basic industries, and social welfare. In foreign policy it means opposing communist revolution, working for disarmament, common prosperity and the prevention of war through international co-operation.²

The party, as we have seen, did not entirely reject the notion of a 'third force', despite its emphasis on collective security. Party spokesmen often talked of 'democratic socialism' as a weapon against war in a way that neither capitalism nor communism, ranged in hostile camps, could hope to be. It could also help liberate Asia from the vestiges of colonial rule, thus further contributing to peace. In this task, Japan was often spoken of as a 'bridge', either between 'free Asia' and 'progressive elements in Western Europe', or more specifically, between the Socialist International and the ASC.³

At the ASC Preliminary Meeting of March 1952 the Right Socialist foreign affairs spokesman Sone Eki rejected 'third force' neutralism and called instead for Asian socialists to support the UN and 'collective security'. The ASC, he maintained, should co-operate closely with the Socialist International. This was also the purport of his remarks at the first plenary session in January 1953 and, as we have seen, the Conference endorsed a final resolution containing substantial concessions to these views.⁴

The RSP clearly regarded the formation of the ASC as an event of great importance, perhaps leading to a progressive international movement in which a democratic socialist Japan could play a prominent part. The core of the party's policy, as seen in its 1953 Action Policy,[5] was the idea of a coalition of European and Asian socialists in the interests of world peace. The general approach of the Socialist International was central to this concept, but a separate organization of Asian socialists could serve as an additional platform for Asian nationalism and thus correct a certain European bias which the Socialist International tended to show.

There is an obvious similarity between these policies and 'third force' ideas current among Left Socialists. The differences, however, were equally important. Neutrality and neutralism, though admitted to be reasonable policies for such countries as India, Indonesia and Burma, were firmly rejected for Japan. Japan's own foreign policy should ideally be based on collective security organized through the UN. Since, however, this ideal was still remote, and in any case Japan was not yet a member of the world body, she had to fall back on regional collective security.

The Right Socialists were most explicit about their dislike of communism, which they thought posed a sufficient threat to Japanese security to rule out the possibility of neutralism. Though they felt this threat was one of internal subversion rather than of external aggression, the mischief-potential of communist countries seemed to them still far from exhausted. There might, indeed, be room for improvement in relations between Japan and her communist neighbours, but the trade advantages likely to accrue from such an amelioration appeared limited. As for the left wing idea of non-aggression treaties linking Japan with the Soviet Union and communist China, the RSP condemned it as a dangerous illusion.[6]

On the recognition of communist China, the party's policy did not remain entirely consistent. The 1952 Action Policy, written when there seemed little immediate prospect of a settlement to the Korean war, said that recognition should be withheld,[7] whereas the Policy for 1953 said that Japan should recognize the Peking régime once the war was over.[8] Interestingly enough—and this was where RSP policy on China came to differ most significantly from the concrete actions of the Japanese government—the party also held that a settlement of the Korean war should precede Japan's recognition of Nationalist China.[9]

The main obscurity in the foreign policy of the Right Socialists concerned Japan's Security Treaty with the United States. As we have seen, the party was strongly anti-communist. It approved the Allied stand in Korea as within the spirit of the UN and supporting world peace. On the other hand neither the 1952 nor the 1953 Action Policy explicitly supported the stationing of American troops in Japan as part of the regional collective security that the party approved in principle. Initially the party had opposed the 1951 Security Treaty on the ground that Japan had not been independent at the time it was concluded. It now spoke of 'renegotiation on equal terms', but the desiderata of such a 'renegotiated' treaty were left unstated.

The obscurity may be traced to two factors operative at the time. One was the attractiveness from the party's point of view of the 'third force' concept (though the actual term was rejected) as an escape from the uncomfortable bipolarity of east-west confrontation. At various times the UN, the Socialist International, the ASC and ICFTU were spoken of as though they were capable, if given the chance, of standing between the two opposed blocs. The other factor was simply the desirability of discovering or manufacturing a foreign policy distinct from those of the parties which flanked the Right Socialists to the left and to the right. This consideration occasionally led them to make apparently hair-splitting distinctions. For instance, on the question of defence, the party acknowledged that Japan as a sovereign nation had the right to defend herself, and that this entitled her to maintain 'defence forces'.[10] The creation of 'defence forces', however, was not the same thing as 'rearmament'. 'Rearmament' implied armed forces capable of combatting a foreign aggressor, while 'defence forces' meant essentially security troops prepared to deal with internal subversion. Only the latter were desirable for Japan. Furthermore, according to the 1953 Action Policy 'the basis of defence is the desire for national independence, economic strength and a secure standard of living.'[11] The party therefore concluded that too much expenditure on defence would itself be prejudicial to security,[12] and made prominent use of the slogan 'Fight for stable living standards rather than rearmament'.

It is obvious that this policy was more complicated (and perhaps less comprehensible to the electorate) than either rearmament within the American alliance or unarmed neutralism. It was complicated because its authors were affected by at least three separate influences. First, anti-communism dictated alliance with the United States, or rearmament, or both. Unlike their left wing rivals, the Right Socialists naturally inclined to a western alignment. Second, however, their memories of what militarism had meant for Japan before 1945, and the prevailing anti-war climate of opinion, inclined them against rearmament as a clear-cut policy. And third, they feared that economic stability and social welfare would be adversely affected by a heavy burden of armaments.

This is, of course, an analysis with one important factor missing. Perhaps not surprisingly a compromise between conflicting motivations was also in part an adjustment of the views of different factions. As among members of the LSP, in the RSP too the question of factional harmony was a crucial one. The difficulties involved in maintaining such harmony proved as great if not greater in the right wing party than in the left.

The first round in a conflict between left and right wings of the RSP came shortly after the party's formation. In March 1952 *Minsharen* (*Minshushakaishugi Remmei*) (Democratic-Socialist League), a supporters' group associated with the right, issued a manifesto supporting rearmament and calling for revision of the Constitution so that rearmament could be carried out constitutionally.[13] This drew a sharp reaction from the Kawakami faction on the left but was endorsed by the Nishio faction on the right. A series of factional manoeuvres led in August of the same year to a 'barter' agreement whereby Kawakami was elected party Chairman in exchange for the readmission to party membership of Nishio, who had been kept out since his alleged part in the 1948 financial scandals which brought down the coalition government.[14]

Kawakami, on appointment, pledged himself to defend the Constitution and oppose rearmament. With his close colleague

Asanuma Inejirō in the second-ranking party post of Secretary-General, the party's left wing seemed to be in a commanding position, although the readmission of Nishio clearly strengthened the right. At any rate the foreign policy already discussed was drawn up by this combination of forces and remained essentially unchallenged until late in 1953.

A serious disagreement was, however, exposed during preparations for the party Congress of January 1954. This sprang from a document drawn up in October 1953 by Sone Eki, the party's Foreign Policy Chairman and a leading Nishio supporter.[15] Sone, a key figure on the party's right wing, put forward three quite new proposals.

The first was that the gradual armaments build-up being conducted by the Yoshida government should be supported. Whereas previous RSP policy had rejected anything more than internal security forces, Sone now proposed support for a policy of rearmament that had progressed to the stage of defence against external attack.

Sone's second proposal was that the existing Security Treaty should be replaced by a new one, temporary in nature, and negotiated 'from an equal standpoint', thus eliminating the clauses considered humiliating for Japan. 'Replacement' was subsequently changed into 'revision', on the grounds, apparently, that a totally new treaty might well involve Japan in new commitments, such as a commitment to send her troops abroad.[16]

This third proposal was the participation of Japanese troops in UN peace-keeping operations. This was of course a logical extension of the party's enthusiasm for the UN, but conflicted with anti-rearmament sentiment and the desire not to be involved in military operations away from home.

Discussion of Sone's proposals quickly revealed the extent to which the party was divided. Predictably, the Nishio faction supported him. The most extreme view was put forward by Nishimura Eiichi, who had previously argued for a form of armed neutrality. He now maintained that the defeat and discrediting of Japan's militarists was an excellent opportunity to build a 'democratic' defence force devoid of fascist overtones.[17] It seems, however, that Nishimura's opinion represented little more than himself. Sone, in defending his draft in committee, was more circumspect, merely submitting that the necessity of armed forces for defence should be clearly stated.[18]

In contrast, the Kawakami faction and its sympathizers opposed hints of rearmament in the Sone proposals. Asanuma came out strongly against any attempt to rewrite the Security Treaty, on the grounds that if perpetuated in any form, it would tend to acquire the characteristics of a 'military alliance'. It was also his view that Japanese participation in UN peace-keeping forces was a Utopian and dangerous idea, implying acceptance of rearmament.[19]

Meanwhile on the left wing of the party another group had been formed with the object of reuniting the party with the LSP. This group, known as the *Chūkanha* (centre faction) countered Sone's *démarche* with an attempt to bring party policy more in line with that of the LSP. It held that not only the Sone draft, but even existing party policy as endorsed by the 1953 Congress had been made obsolete by events on the international stage during that same year. The Soviet peace offensive, the increased influence of small nations at the UN, and the sharpening isolation of the United States made it pointless to continue talking about America as the bulwark of world peace, or of the danger of Soviet and communist Chinese aggression. The group therefore called for efforts towards a peace treaty with those ex-belligerents who had not signed at San Francisco, and for total abolition of the 1951 Security Treaty.[20]

This intra-party debate continued until the Congress of January 1954. The Nishio faction and the *Chūkanha* continued to press their respective cases. In the end the issue was effectively decided by the Kawakami faction whose success since 1952 in dominating key party positions made it the most vital factor in the situation. Shortly before the Congress Kawakami himself, as party Chairman, made a major policy speech attacking, in terms stronger than had been used officially by the party before, the current defence policy of the government. Japan, he is reported to have said, had no further need to defend herself against external aggression, and in the developing world situation the United States would have to switch from military alliances to economic aid if she were to be able to compete with the Soviet peace offensive.[21]

The foreign policy resolution finally agreed upon by the Congress contained certain concessions to the Nishio faction, but its general policy line was oriented rather towards the party's left wing. On the question of the Security Treaty it differed little from the 1953 Action Policy, starting from the ideal of UN 'collective security', but admitting, in default of this, the necessity of regional security arrangements. It advocated revision of the 'inequalities' of the 1951 Security Treaty without saying anything either about the status of the Treaty or about the stationing of American troops in Japan. A permanent UN police force was also suggested, but the question of Japan's participation in it was not mentioned.[22]

On the problem of defence the 1954 Policy was more specific than that of 1953 although a similar line was followed. What in 1953 had been defined and approved as an 'internal security force against subversion' was now specifically pegged at the size of the Police Reserve set up by General MacArthur in 1950. (This force reached 70,000 men.) The Nishio faction received a minor concession in that a defence force against direct aggression was stated to be 'theoretically' possible. On the other hand the government's military build-up was roundly condemned as a violation of the Constitution, a danger to democracy and potentially destructive of the economic stability that was the real basis of defence. The point that economic stability would remove the danger of subversion, and that any form of rearmament should at least be postponed until a strong economy and a fair division of its products had been brought about, was stressed at length.[23]

This resolution, in view of the fierce controversy it aroused at the Congress, must be seen as merely an interim statement of what could be agreed, masking points of disagreement with obscurity or silence. The controversy between the two wings of the party continued, and now came to centre upon the negotiations for reunification with the Left Socialists.

It is interesting to compare the records of the two parties in their respective attempts to project a coherent foreign policy. Both parties, being composed of disparate factions, underwent serious difficulties in formulating that policy. The Left Socialists, as we have seen, found their 'third force' neutralism challenged by their own left wing. That challenge, however, was successfully withstood. The Right Socialists, in contrast, failed to agree on a foreign policy that would be more than a compromise between incompatibles. The reasons must be sought in factional history and ideological background.

The Kawakami and Nishio factions had a long record of rivalry. In the 1930s the faction now led by Kawakami had generally overshadowed the Nishio faction and thus controlled the *Shakai Taishūtō*, leading that party into close co-operation with the militarists. As a result, most of the faction's leaders had been purged after the war making it possible for the Nishio faction to dominate the revived socialist movement. Once the Kawakami faction's leaders were depurged, they found themselves once more confronting their old rivals in a party composed almost entirely of right wing and moderate socialists. It may not be fanciful to suggest that the anti-rearmament stand now taken by the Kawakami faction sprang in part from its desire to erase the taint of its pre-war association with the militarists—a constraint which did not affect the Nishio faction to the same degree.

The task of creating a foreign policy that would satisfy both these groups and also the newly formed *Chūkanha* was obviously difficult, a harder task, indeed, than that confronting the Left Socialists. For one thing the *Rōnō-ha* tradition with its deep historical roots and capacity to unite a large section of the Marxist left, did not have its counterpart in the RSP. 'Democratic socialism' had shallower roots in Japan, and concealed differences dating from before World War II. Moreover, the Left Socialist 'third force' neutralism had the advantage of clarity. It was presented as a distinct alternative between the two poles of a pro-communist and a pro-western foreign policy. The Right Socialists, on the other hand, were faced with the more delicate problem of delineating a foreign policy in between support for the west and neutralism. When such a policy, replete with compromises and evasions, was finally decided upon it proved insufficiently attractive to prevent the rival groups within the party from gravitating towards the more clear-cut policies of parties flanking them to their right and left respectively.

As was the case with the LSP, the RSP was influenced by international events following upon the death of Stalin in February 1953. Since the Japanese socialist movement had split in 1951 over a disagreement about security against communism, a relaxation of world tension strengthened the hand of those who said Japan did not need to rearm and did not need a defensive alliance. It thus brightened the prospects for reunification, if the RSP was willing to accept this. It was this path that the Kawakami faction, spearheaded by the *Chūkanha,* now determined to take.

7

REUNIFICATION

In October 1955 Left and Right Socialist Parties united under their old name, the Japan Socialist Party. Thus ended more than two difficult years of bargaining over policy, ideology and party posts. A clash of opinion over the peace settlement and its provisions for the security of Japan had been the occasion for the 1951 split, and these problems also proved the most intractable in 1955. The result was a painful compromise between conflicting views. Nevertheless, the fact that a settlement was actually reached shows that much had changed between 1951 and 1955, even if the parties' response to those changes was slow and rather grudging.

Serious and hopeful discussions between the two parties did not begin until April 1954, when two top officials from each party met as a four-man committee to work out a basis for reunification. The first indication of positive thinking on the subject had come in July 1953, in a speech by the LSP Chairman Suzuki Mosaburō.[1] Shortly afterwards, the LSP set up a 'reunification committee', and the Right Socialist *Chūkanha* pamphlet came remarkably close to Left Socialist positions on the vital issues of defence, neutralism and the 'third force'.[2] It said that rearmament should be opposed at all costs, called for 'self-reliant neutralism' (a Left Socialist term) and agreed that the RSP had much to learn from 'third force' ideas put forward by the LSP. This positive approach, however, did not immediately commend itself to either of the other Right Socialist factions.[3]

Meanwhile, in the LSP a foreign policy statement of September 1953 contained two significant policy changes. The statement indicated that the party, while still demanding abolition of the Security Treaty and Administrative Agreement, was prepared to accept the Peace Treaty provided only that certain military clauses were deleted from it. The second change was of great potential importance. One of the main objections continually levelled by the Right Socialists against neutralism was that it neglected security and would render Japan defenceless against an aggressor. This was why they had always favoured some form of collective security. To meet such criticism, the Left Socialists now proposed that the security of a neutral, unarmed Japan should be guaranteed by a treaty of non-aggression between her and 'countries concerned, in the area of Japan'.[4]

This idea was inspired by Churchill's speech to the House of Commons of 11 May 1953, in which he called for a treaty to guarantee the eastern frontiers of Germany and the western frontiers of the Soviet Union, on the model of the 1925 Treaty of Locarno. (The Locarno Treaty had included as its main item a mutual guarantee of the frontiers of France and Belgium by Germany, Belgium, France, Great Britain and Italy.)

The application of the 'Locarno' concept to Japan meant of course a treaty of non-aggression between communist and noncommunist countries; specifically it included Japan, the Soviet Union, communist China and the United States.

Although the idea was to prove the basis for eventual reconciliation between Left and Right Socialists, the initial reaction of the RSP was unfavourable. An RSP committee set up in September 1953 to consider problems of reunification (the initiative seems to have come from the *Chūkanha* but representatives of all factions participated) criticized the LSP for including the Soviet Union and communist China as guarantors of Japan's security. The committee connected this apparent change from 'self-reliant neutralism' to 'guaranteed neutralism' with the 'peace forces' argument currently raging among the Left Socialists, and alleged that the LSP had in effect capitulated to the supporters of the 'peace forces'.[5]

By April 1954, however, when the above-mentioned four-man discussions began, the Right Socialist objections to a 'Locarno' solution had been more or less assuaged. The most important achievement of these talks was that the representatives of both sides were able to agree, at least in principle, to this plan. This meant that for the first time a means had been found of bridging the gap between Left Socialist neutralism and Right Socialist collective security. Nevertheless, the two sides differed widely in their respective interpretations of how such a treaty should be brought about. The LSP negotiators thought that separate mutual non-aggression treaties should be concluded between Japan and the Soviet Union, Japan and communist China, and Japan and the United States. At some unspecified date after such a network of treaties had been concluded, it should be capped with an overall treaty embracing all four powers. According to this view, the 'Locarno' solution was to *replace* both the Japan-United States Security Treaty and the Sino-Soviet Treaty of Friendship. The RSP negotiators, on the other hand, thought that a four-power treaty should not replace, but supplement, the existing security arrangements that each bloc had in the Far East.[6]

This difference in interpretation reflected the fundamentally different stands of the two parties—if the Security Treaty were abolished as a pre-condition of a four-power treaty, the Left Socialist aim of neutralism for Japan would have thereby been fulfilled. If, on the other hand, a four-power treaty were achieved without the prior nullification of the Security Treaty then the Right Socialist requirement of 'collective security' would have been met.[7]

Another important task for the four-man committee was to reconcile the views of the two parties on defence. Some compromise had to be found between the LSP insistence on total abolition of what were now termed the 'Self-Defence Forces', and the RSP policy that an internal security force for use against subversion, not exceeding in size that of the Police Reserve Force of 1950, be maintained.

Despite these advances, the factional situation in each party prevented further progress for the time being. Among the Right Socialists the Nishio faction remained hostile to attempts at unification. Nishio himself warned against 'unprincipled' unification and hinted that the Constitution should be revised to permit rearmament.[8] This statement drew a sharp reaction from Kōno Mitsu, of the Kawakami faction, a strong advocate of unity.[9] Nishio and Kōno were old rivals within the socialist

movement. This was partly because of membership of factions
which had been rivals since 1926, and partly because of a violent
personal quarrel between the two men in 1938, as a result of
which Kōno was instrumental in having Nishio expelled from
the Imperial Diet.

In the LSP the Suzuki faction (which controlled the party
Chairmanship and other key positions) was the spearhead of
the 'reunification' group and was probably backed at this stage
by the small Nomizo faction.[10] The factional harmony noted in
chapter 5 between the Suzuki and Wada factions apparently
did not survive the decision by the former to seek reunification.[11]
The reluctance of the Wada faction to go along with Suzuki in
this enterprise was motivated less by ideological differences,
which were slight or non-existent, than by the sheer logic of
relations between the various factions. The Wada faction probably feared a plot by the Suzuki and Kawakami factions—the
most powerful groups in the LSP and RSP respectively—to
exclude it from a fair share of power in the reunited party.[12]
The only LSP faction to oppose reunification on specifically
ideological grounds was the ultra-leftist Matsumoto faction,
which did, however, enjoy much less backing among the Left
Socialists than did the Nishio faction among the Right Socialists.

Curiously enough, although the committed opponents of reunification were at this point rather less significant in the LSP
than in the RSP, it was in the LSP that the outcome of the
four-man talks met the more hostile reaction. Itō Kōdō—one
of the Left Socialist negotiators and a strong supporter of reunification—stated publicly that defence forces restricted to an
anti-subversion role and preferably termed 'police forces' might
be acceptable to his party.[13] This provoked another leading Left
Socialist, Okada Sōji, to call for reunification of the two parties
on specifically Left Socialist terms. Okada uncompromisingly
urged complete abolition of the existing Self-Defence Forces,
and denied any possibility of Soviet or Chinese aggression against
Japan.[14] This statement seems to have been primarily a bargaining manoeuvre designed to pressure the Right Socialists into
accepting reunification on terms advantageous to the LSP.
Okada no doubt realized that with his party overtaking the
Right Socialists electorally, and with the prospects of Soviet or

Chinese aggression against Japan having obviously faded, the bargaining position of the Right Socialists had weakened.[15]

In October 1954 a delegation from both socialist parties visited communist China. The RSP part of the delegation included both Kōno Mitsu, who championed the cause of reunification, and Sone Eki, who had hitherto opposed it. The report which these members presented on their return to their Central Executive Committee differed significantly on several issues from the previous party line. For instance, they took a much more favourable view of communist China. Previously, the party had supported the UN condemnation of the Peking government for its part in the Korean war and had said that recognition of both Chinas should be withheld. With the settlement of that war the party began to advocate recognition of Peking, provided communist China agreed to the 'democratic' unification and neutralization of the Korean peninsula.[16]

The delegation's report now said that awakened nationalism was more important in China than Marx-Leninism. The Chinese people were essentially peaceful, and sincerely wanted peaceful co-existence with the rest of the world in order to devote themselves to the tasks of peaceful economic development. China was right in promoting neutralism among her smaller and weaker neighbours, and might perhaps prove an important countervailing force in Asia against possible Soviet pretensions.[17]

Arguing from these premises the report put forward a number of concrete policies for Japan: the Taiwan question should be settled on the principle that the island should return to China (a notable departure, this, from previous policy),[18] restrictions on Japan-China trade should be abolished, and a pact of non-aggression and non-interference should be concluded between Japan and China (if possible as part of a four-power treaty).[19]

That a member of the *Chūkanha* or Kawakami faction should have written a report of this nature in a year when the Geneva Conference had ended the Indochina war, and when communist China was trying to convince the uncommitted Asian nations of the sincerity of her 'peaceful co-existence' would scarcely have seemed surprising. The fact, however, that Sone, the foreign affairs expert of the Nishio faction, should have lent his name to such a report, was of great importance for the future of the reunification negotiations.

The Right Socialist Central Executive Committee debated the report with some heat. It was welcomed by the factions favouring reunification but opposed by leaders of the Nishio faction, especially Nishio himself, and was therefore shelved.[20]

At about the same time both parties were attempting to draw up a common platform on which to fight the 1955 general elections, and this was to be used as a 'test run' for unification. In November 1954 a platform was formulated, although it only papered over certain real divisions. It also embodied some substantial concessions by the Left Socialists. As we have seen already, the two parties differed in their interpretations of a hypothetical four-power treaty over the question of what to do with the existing Security Treaty. The Right Socialists insisted it should be retained, pending either effective collective security by the UN or a four-power treaty, but that in the meantime its 'inequalities' should be revised. The Left Socialists simply said it should be abolished. The gap was bridged by a mere verbal trick. The first character of the word for 'revise' (*kaitei*) was combined with the first character of the word for 'abolish' (*haishi*) to make a word which might be rendered 'revise-abolish' (*kaihai*), so that the policy read 'revise-abolish unequal treaties'.[21]

On defence, the LSP made an important concession by qualifying its previous insistence on immediate demobilization of the Self-Defence Forces, and agreeing that their numbers should be decreased gradually. It also agreed to the following clause, which seemed to endorse at least the principles of defence: 'We aim to guarantee the standard of living of the people, the realization of a just society, and the establishment of a peaceful independent economy, in order thus to build the basis of defence.'[22]

After the general elections of February 1955 both parties showed greater confidence in their ability to reunite, and negotiations between them began in earnest in May and lasted until September. As a result of the election, both socialist parties gained seats and achieved for the first time the one third of Lower House seats necessary to block constitutional revision, while the LSP still further increased its lead over the RSP.[23] Perhaps because of this Left Socialist success the Wada faction, hitherto cautious about unity, and the Matsumoto faction, which had been directly opposed to it, apparently moved in favour.[24] All the party's factions (especially the Matsumoto faction) had done well in the election, and thus felt themselves able both to make their policies felt in the unified platform and to dominate a reunited party.

The first round in the 1955 negotiations was fired by the Left Socialist Chairman Suzuki, who criticized a draft platform which had been prepared by the Right Socialists.[25] His objection was essentially ideological: the draft stated that Japan, despite the Security Treaty, was 'independent' of the United States. Suzuki objected that she was a 'subordinate country' controlled by both Japanese capital and American imperialism, and therefore it was incorrect to say she was independent.[26] The authenticity of Suzuki's remarks was subsequently denied,[27] and it seems that this episode, which caused considerable ill-feeling, was part of a Left Socialist campaign to drive a harder bargain.

As before, the vexed questions of defence and rearmament played a critical part in the discussions. The Left Socialist negotiators eventually made the concession that their party would reconsider the question 'if at some future time the establishment of armed forces were recognized to be necessary'.[28] For the benefit of their own party members they then issued a reassurance that this would be unlikely if, as might be expected, international tensions continued to relax.[29] One leading party member was also quoted as saying that a future re-examination of the rearmament issue was out of the question.[30]

Meanwhile the Right Socialists still insisted on some minimal defence preparedness, while continuing to emphasize the importance of a prosperous economy as the best guarantee of national security—a view which the Left Socialists had accepted for the purposes of the joint election platform. Most significantly, however, the 'pro-unification' factions in the RSP now swung closer to acceptance of neutralism, although they used rather different language. Thus, for instance, Kōno Mitsu said that he opposed neutralism but supported a foreign policy based on self-reliant independence and non-involvement in war. He commended such nations as Yugoslavia, Austria and India as the nucleus of a peace bloc which might successfully relax international tension.[31]

The unification committee finally hammered out an agreed platform containing many hard-fought compromises.[32] On the surface its foreign policy section appeared to be a victory for the Right rather than the Left. 'Neutralism' and 'third force' were not mentioned, but the Right Socialist term 'self-reliant independence' was made the keystone of the unified party's foreign policy. The basic aims of this policy were stated to be: 'to achieve total independence for Japan, to preserve international peace and security in her area, to make her economically independent, and thus create friendly relations with all other nations from the standpoint of self-reliant independence with regard to either camp.'[33]

Nevertheless, the Left Socialist promoters of the new platform could plausibly argue in the face of criticism from their own ranks that the platform gave to the LSP the substance of its original neutralist policy while taking away the name.[34] Although the platform did not mention neutralism, its articles on security and defence were capable of wide interpretation. In particular they contained the stated aim of a 'Locarno' treaty, upon which the compromise over national security was founded. This section of the agreed platform is crucial enough for us to reproduce it here in full:

(1) *Security*

The Security envisaged for Japan shall be as follows:

(a) We shall attempt to obtain non-aggression agreements with all the countries concerned in the area around Japan, especially communist China and the Soviet Union, and to conclude a collective treaty of non-aggression and security, in which the main participants will be the United States, the Soviet Union and communist China.

(b) In consideration of a collective security treaty in which both camps would participate, the Security Treaty and Administrative Agreement between Japan and the United States should be dissolved, and simultaneously the Sino-Soviet Treaty of Friendship should be dissolved.

(2) *Defence*

(a) We oppose present rearmament.

(b) We shall attempt to prevent the build-up of the Self-Defence Forces and shall seek gradually to reduce them.

(c) We shall give ultimate support for the United Nations and a UN police force, after international disarmament is implemented.

(d) We shall organize a democratic and mobile police system to maintain internal security.[35]

The significant ambiguity in the 'Locarno' policy was that the stage at which existing security arrangements were to be 'dissolved' was nowhere mentioned. This left it open to Left Socialists to make their own interpretation emphasizing abolition of the Security Treaty, while the Right Socialists could make this dependent on the prior establishment of a four-power treaty.

It will also be observed that the platform glossed over the question of defence forces. This was fully recognized by opponents of reunification at the LSP Congress held in September 1955. The Left Socialist leadership had to defend itself against the charge that the phrase 'we oppose present rearmament' did not necessarily imply opposition to future rearmament.[36] This, however, was a concession to the Right Socialist demand that the door should not be closed to rearmament in future contingencies. This Left Socialist Congress in fact revealed a surprising amount of opposition to the agreement that had been hammered out between the two parties. The Matsumoto faction in particular, though it had earlier come round to supporting reunification in principle, now attacked the agreed platform for its concessions to the 'Rightists', especially in regard to security and rearmament.[37] More surprisingly the faction was joined in its stand by the *Shakaishugi Kyōkai*. The ideological quarrel in 1953 between this group of intellectuals and the Matsumoto faction has already been described. An alliance between them to block unification at this late hour was well calculated to produce the maximum effect. They now presented to the Congress a resolution calling for the complete abandonment of the agreed platform as a basis for unification.

Although the resolution was defeated, its supporters mustered a staggering proportion of about one third of the votes cast.[38] This result was very shocking to the Left Socialist leadership and also to the Right Socialists, whose central committee resolved that the agreed platform must be passed unanimously at the reunification congress due in October.

Mutual recriminations continued right up till the reunification congress itself, and the opening of the Congress was delayed twelve hours because of differences over the distribution of party posts. Once the Congress had begun, however, the platform was passed without opposition.

It seems surprising that the Socialists should have found it so difficult to reconcile their foreign policies at this stage. 1954 and 1955 were, after all, years in which international tensions were widely thought to be lessening. They were years which witnessed the Bandung Conference, the settlement of the war in Indochina and the Austrian State Treaty of 15 May 1955 (which provided for the neutralization of Austria). Thus the external situation seemed to differ greatly from that of 1951 when the JSP split. In these circumstances the electoral attractions of something approaching a neutralist foreign policy were considerable. The fear of communism had receded.

Again, on the domestic scene the so-called 'reverse course' which the Yoshida government had pursued after Japan regained her independence was deeply disquieting to most progressive thinkers. The dismantling of Occupation reforms in education, labour relations, anti-trust legislation and local government, and especially the creation of the Self-Defence Forces with American aid under the Mutual Security Assistance Agreement, led to fears that the government intended to revise the Constitution as a prelude to the reimposition of 'feudal' rule. Obvious American support for the Japanese government thus tended to weaken the appeal of collective defence on behalf of the 'free world'. It should be noted that even the right wing Nishio faction did not advocate more than token rearmament and did not call for unconditional support for the Peace Treaty settlement.

A further motive for unification, absent in 1951, existed in 1954 and 1955. Divisions among the various conservative parties, the protracted refusal of Yoshida to resign as Prime Minister despite increasing pressure upon him to do so, the eventual collapse of his government, continued divisions under the Hatoyama government in 1955, and Socialist gains at successive elections, made it seem not impossible that a united socialist party might soon be in a position to form a majority government.[39] Parallel moves in the conservative camp to unite its various factions (which were to result in December 1955 in the formation of the Liberal-Democratic Party) made the problem of socialist unity seem doubly urgent.

Why then were the negotiations, especially over national security and the maintenance of armed forces, so long and difficult?

The reason lies mainly in the ideological and factional nature of the debate. The Right Socialist Nishio faction and the Left Socialist Matsumoto faction both had strong ideological views and stood their ground. The Nishio faction was strongly anti-communist—an attitude probably derived from its experiences in the non-Marxist wing of the socialist movement in the late 1920s—and was therefore sharply suspicious of pro-communist tendencies in the LSP. At the other extreme the Matsumoto faction was extremely hostile to any Right Socialist proposal which could be interpreted as a move in the direction of rearmament or of a closer alignment with the United States.

The 'reunification group' within the LSP also had a clearly defined ideological position from which it was reluctant to move. During the 1955 negotiations its concessions on defence seem to have been tactical, and each concession had to be followed up with an elaborate explanation to the party. No doubt its concessions were made in the confident belief that the essence of a neutralist foreign policy was still being retained. In the end, however, the compromise did not prove acceptable to its own ideological purists in the *Shakaishugi Kyōkai*.

The Right Socialist 'reunification group' was in a position permitting greater flexibility than that of any other group in either party. Its leaders were agreed that a degree of support for the 'free world' was desirable, and accepted the necessity at least in principle of collective security, but held that Japan was not yet completely independent and that she should substantially loosen her ties with the United States. In response to the pressure of negotiations and because of their quarrels with the Nishio faction, they were prepared to make substantial concessions towards a neutralist foreign policy.

The task of reuniting in one party both extremists and moderates on both sides could only have been accomplished provided that the anti-communism of the Nishio faction and the anti-American anti-rearmament sentiment of the Matsumoto faction were satisfied. The moderate factions dominant in each party finally achieved a solution on this basis for two reasons: the 'third force' neutralism of the Left Socialist 'reunification group' had been shown to be opposed to alliance with communism; and the 'self-reliant independence' of the Right Socialist 'reunification group' was basically opposed to rearmament and a consolidation of the American alliance.

It required, however, a combination of favourable circumstances to bring the long-drawn-out negotiations to a successful conclusion.

8

SUZUKI, ASANUMA AND
'POSITIVE NEUTRALITY'

For the first three years after reunification Left and Right in the new party coexisted on the basis of the agreed platform. This platform, as we have seen, made no mention of neutralism, but used instead the term 'self-reliant independence'. Although this was a considerable *verbal* concession to the Right Socialists, the Left Socialists had made few concessions of substance in matters of foreign policy and defence.[1]

In January 1959, however, the party proclaimed a foreign policy based on what was termed 'positive neutrality'. When spelled out in detail, the new policy did not seem so very different from that which had gone before and most of the changes were clearly derived from new elements in the international situation. It included, for instance, a new emphasis on nuclear disarmament which was obviously introduced because of the increased number and refinement of nuclear weapons (and their means of delivery) in the hands of the two major powers.[2] Nevertheless, the change of name from 'self-reliant independence' to 'positive neutrality' was symbolically significant in that it meant reversion to a terminology associated with the Left rather than the Right. It was also part of a gradual drift to the left of the party as a whole.

Immediately after reunification, policies of a more or less neutralist colouring were acceptable even to former Right Socialists.[3] The Suez and Hungary crises of October-November 1956 temporarily renewed cold war tensions, but Japan's entry into the UN in December encouraged the party to think that Japan (presumably under a socialist government) might use the UN as a forum for the expression of an independent voice in world affairs—the voice of a 'member of the Asian and African group, working for the peace of Asia and the world'.[4] This of course was a period when the 'Bandung spirit' was still widely discussed. Japanese Socialists officially regarded the Bandung Conference of April 1955 as having served to increase the international importance of the non-aligned nations of Asia and Africa. They cited, for instance, the role played by the UN and the Afro-Asian group in bringing the Suez affair to a conclusion.[5]

No party faction at this stage dissented from these general views, but in questions closer to home than Suez right wing and left wing opinions tended to diverge substantially. One such question was the current negotiations between Japan and the Soviet Union. Restoration of diplomatic relations with the Soviet Union and the signature of a peace treaty between the two countries was the most important self-appointed task of the Hatoyama government (1955–6). In this aim Hatoyama had the backing of the Socialists, who had long deplored the absence of formal Soviet-Japanese relations and regretted that the San Francisco Peace Treaty was of such a nature that the Soviet Union had refused to sign it. The settlement which Hatoyama finally concluded in November 1956, after long and difficult negotiations, stopped short of a peace treaty but re-established diplomatic relations.

The most intractable problem which faced the negotiators was the territorial issue. In 1945 the Soviet Union had taken possession of the southern half of the island of Sakhalin and of the whole Kurile chain including some small islands off the coast of Hokkaidō (Habomai and Shikotan) which had been administered before 1945 as part of Hokkaidō. Japan was now seeking the return of her sovereignty over at least part of this territory; in the end she was content to claim only the southern-most Kuriles, as well as Habomai and Shikotan. By the terms of the 1956 settlement the Soviet Union agreed to return these last-named islands as soon as a peace treaty were signed (the 1955–6 negotiations failed to achieve one) but no agreement at all was reached on the South Kuriles.

Although a settlement with the Soviet Union was an important item in the JSP's foreign policy, the party was divided over its attitudes to the actual negotiations. Former Left Socialists were generally prepared to accept territorial concessions for the sake of a peace treaty, and maintained that Japan should be prepared to relinquish her claim to the South Kuriles if it were necessary for that end. Former Right Socialists, on the other hand, were less prepared to concede 'Japanese territory'.[6]

The party was also far from united over the China issue. The 1955 reunification platform called for the restoration of relations with communist China (as well as with the Soviet Union). On the most difficult part of the China problem—the status of Taiwan—the platform merely said that a peaceful settlement of international tension over Taiwan should be negotiated.[7] This was a compromise formula: the Left had held that Nationalist China should no longer be recognized and that a decision on the return of Taiwan to China should be made at a referendum of all Chinese inhabitants of both the mainland and Taiwan; the Right, on the other hand, had supported a 'two Chinas' formula as a provisional solution, while admitting that Taiwan should eventually return to China; meanwhile, it argued, the inhabitants of Taiwan alone should be allowed to state their views in a referendum.[8]

The compromise, however, did not prove a stable one and in May 1956 the JSP central committee adopted, against the Nishio faction's opposition, a resolution condemning proposals either for UN control of Taiwan or for a referendum of its inhabitants, as unwarranted interference in China's domestic affairs, and declaring Taiwan an integral part of China.[9]

Once the Japan-Soviet agreement was signed the JSP began an all out campaign to restore diplomatic relations with Peking. The early months of 1957 were notable for intensive Chinese efforts for recognition and for the short-lived Ishibashi government which was more or less sympathetic towards them. It was in this atmosphere that the JSP drew up its 1957 Action Policy which called for a broad popular movement under Socialist leadership but including those businessmen who were keen to trade with China. At the same time the JSP made a slight break with previous policy by announcing that it was prepared to co-operate with the JCP in mass campaigns for specific aims (such as recognition of Peking) but still did not wish to enter a general-purpose alliance or united front.[10] This move was influenced by the more flexible line of the JCP following its sixth national Congress in July 1956. At this Congress the Communists had formally abandoned their underground and paramilitary activities (now styled 'ultra-leftist adventurism') in which they had indulged since the Cominform criticism of January 1950. They now called upon all 'progressive forces'— including the Socialists—to join them in the struggle against American 'imperialism'.

As part of its China campaign the JSP in April 1957 sent a delegation (the first sent by the united party) to Peking. On the eve of its departure the party issued a statement of policy confirming in stronger language the trend leftwards evident since the declaration of May 1956. 'China is one', it proclaimed, 'and Taiwan is part of China. We do not recognize the existence of two Chinas.'[11] In Peking, the delegation confirmed this stand in a joint statement with its Chinese hosts, and called for relations between the two countries to be restored.[12]

Meanwhile considerable progress had been made towards closer trading links between Japan and communist China. The third unofficial trade agreement, negotiated in May 1955 between the Chinese communists and an unofficial Japanese trade delegation (which had tacit government backing) was renewed in October 1956 for a further year. Such unofficial contacts were regarded fairly sympathetically by the Hatoyama and Ishibashi governments. When, however, in February 1957 Kishi replaced Ishibashi as Prime Minister, the attitude of the Japanese government began to change. Although Kishi was prepared to permit relaxation of existing embargoes which restricted trade with Peking, his coolness towards communist China soon began to make itself felt. In July 1957 he paid an official visit to Taiwan, an act which the communist Chinese leaders chose to regard with particular hostility.[13]

Trade negotiations, still on an unofficial basis, now began to bog down in unprecedented difficulties. A fourth unofficial trade agreement was finally concluded in March 1958, but only after numerous obstacles had been overcome. This agreement included a very significant provision for the exchange of permanent trade missions, which had the unfortunate effect, from the Japanese

WAYNESBURG COLLEGE LIBRARY
WAYNESBURG, PA.

government's point of view, of seeming to imply some measure of official recognition. Nationalist China consequently attempted to apply pressure on Japan, and a dispute developed about whether the communist Chinese trade mission should be allowed to fly its own national flag. The crisis point came in May of the same year when the communist Chinese flag flying over their trade mission in Nagasaki was hauled down by a Japanese youth. Peking reacted immediately with an order to suspend all trade with Japan.

Stunned by this blow to its hopes for better relations with communist China, the JSP proceeded to lay most of the blame at the door of Kishi and his allegedly 'tough' international line.[14] Now indeed the Socialists confronted a Prime Minister whose foreign policy was opposed to theirs on almost every issue, and this naturally inclined them to greater intransigence.

At this point an even more important political issue was in the making. A few months after her China trade link was severed, Japan embarked upon a course that was to lead to her greatest political crisis since 1945. The Japanese government had good reason to wish to rewrite the Japan-United States Security Treaty which had come into force when Japan regained her independence in 1952. The Treaty had been drawn up when Japan had not yet regained her sovereignty and she had, in a sense, acted under duress. In addition, a number of clauses in the Treaty were widely considered to be to Japan's disadvantage. If a more favourable treaty could be obtained by Japan as a completely sovereign nation, the Japanese government would have won a considerable diplomatic victory.

The Socialists, however, saw things otherwise. No revision of the Security Treaty, however favourable to Japan's interests, could satisfy their demand for its total abolition. The Americans, they argued, wished to use Japan as a nuclear base, strengthening the American strategic position in the Far East by the creation of a *de facto* 'North-East Asia Treaty Organization', embracing besides Japan the Philippines, Taiwan and South Korea. Japan would have to continue to violate flagrantly her own Constitution in order to furnish military assistance to the United States. Although the revised Treaty was to include a clause providing for 'prior consultation' between the governments of Japan and the United States in case a threat developed to the security of Japan or the Far East, this was of little value to Japan unless she could veto American plans. Considering indeed the degree to which the present government was subservient to American wishes, the 'prior consultation' clause might well be used to legitimize the introduction of nuclear weapons onto Japanese soil. The Soviet Union and communist China would undoubtedly consider the Treaty provocative, thus increasing tension in the Far East. Afro-Asian sentiment would also be alienated. The presence of nuclear weapons on Japanese soil would make her the likely target for a pre-emptive nuclear attack. Finally, Japan would be required to increase her armed forces thus increasing the burden of armaments borne by her people and imperilling democratic government.

There was nothing very new in the Socialist position on the Security Treaty, except that the Kishi government's initiative presented them with the unwelcome prospect of a reinvigorated alliance with the United States. This, coupled with the débâcle over trade with communist China, gave an added urgency to their campaigns.[15]

Communist China, meanwhile, was conducting her own campaign against revision of the Security Treaty. Her precipitate severance of trade with Japan was probably partly designed— ineffectually as it transpired—to turn the Japanese voters against Kishi in the May 1958 Lower House general elections. On 19 November 1958 the Chinese Foreign Minister, Chen Yi, in a major speech, called for an end to the Security Treaty in order that Japan should be able to establish what he termed 'peaceful neutrality'.[16] This was followed two weeks later by a similar call from the Soviet Foreign Minister Gromyko. The call for neutralism in these statements apparently struck a receptive chord in the JSP, whose central committee a month later officially declared that the party's foreign policy was one of 'positive neutrality'.

'Positive neutrality' was said to mean four things: non-participation in military blocs, non-interference in the cold war, positive efforts to relax international tension, and peaceful co-existence with all countries. If Japan were to implement these policies they could be expected to bring her true independence, peace and security, while contributing to the relaxation of tension in Asia. Japan's international prestige would rise accordingly.[17] Essentially, this policy differed little from the type of neutralism propounded by the Left Socialists between 1952 and 1955. A similar contrast was pointedly made between neutralism and the 'old-fashioned', 'negative' neutrality of countries such as Switzerland. A similar importance was attached to the desirability of breaking down the dangerous bipolarity in world affairs and of finding a viable alternative to the Security Treaty. Sections of the party's left wing did not attempt to conceal the connection between its new policy and the Chen Yi and Gromyko statements, nor did they deny that 'positive neutrality' represented a move to the left.[18]

Two items in the new policy, however, were of recent origin and reflected a changed international and domestic situation. One was that Japan should make a unilateral declaration banning nuclear weapons from Japanese soil. The other was the related idea that she should work for a nuclear-free zone in the Far East. As formulated in the 1959 Action Policy, the nuclear-free zone was to cover an area of Asia and the northern Pacific including territory belonging to the United States, the Soviet Union, China and Korea.[19] The origin of these proposals was the 1957 Rapacki Plan for the nuclear disengagement of NATO and Warsaw Pact forces from most of central Europe,[20] and they also showed the extent to which concern was now felt within the party about the dangers of introducing nuclear weapons into Japan. In part, this derived from the anti-nuclear feeling that had swept Japan following the *Lucky Dragon* incident of March 1954, when a Japanese fishing boat had been showered with radioactive ash from an American hydrogen bomb test at Bikini Atoll. The following year saw the foundation of *Gensuikyō* (the Japan Council against Atomic and Hydrogen Weapons) which over a period of two years claimed to have collected nearly forty million signatures to a petition calling for a ban on nuclear weapons. (Initially *Gensuikyō* was a non-partisan body, but from about 1958 it began to acquire an increasingly left wing character.)

During the late 1950s the possibility of nuclear weapons being brought into Japan—whether for the American or Japanese forces—became a major bone of contention between the government and the socialists. The introduction in August 1955 for the American forces of Honest-John missiles caused widespread concern, since it was known that these missiles could be fitted with nuclear warheads. The issue arose again in January 1958 when the Japan-United States Security Committee decided that American Sidewinder missiles without nuclear warheads should be provided for the Self-Defence forces. Although there was no concrete evidence that any nuclear weapon had ever been brought into Japan, Socialists and others frequently expressed themselves dissatisfied with government assurances on the matter, citing alleged American statements that the introduction of nuclear weapons and nuclear-tipped missiles was under active consideration.[21] One probable reason for increased socialist interest in the nuclear issue at this time was that all American land combat troops had been withdrawn from Japan by the end of 1957. This considerably reduced the amount of land requisitioned for American bases, and thus removed some of the point from the party's campaign against the bases, which had occupied much of its energies during 1956.

The idea of a nuclear-free zone was indeed new, but it bore a certain similarity to the 'third force' aspect of the earlier neutralism of the Left Socialists. One writer, for instance, thought such a zone would serve to extend the 'central belt' of neutralist Arab and Asian countries into the Far East. If the United States and the Soviet Union disengaged in Europe, there would be a neutral (or at least nuclear-free) zone extending through all the major areas of cold war tension which would lessen the risk of nuclear war, especially arising from local incidents.[22]

It should be noted in passing that shortly before the JSP turned to 'positive neutrality', the JCP had also officially endorsed a policy of neutralism. As we have seen, the parties were on somewhat better terms than they had been before 1957. The Chinese communists, in calling for a neutral Japan, may have calculated that they could thereby promote a united front of Communists and Socialists against the Kishi government. In the event most Socialists rejected the Communist conversion to neutralism as insincere,[23] but nevertheless co-operated with them in the subsequent campaign against revision of the Security Treaty. The Communists left no doubt about the aim of their 'neutralism', specifically stating that it was directed against the United States and the Security Treaty.[24]

'Positive neutrality' was shortly to be subjected to a practical test. In March 1959 a second JSP delegation visited communist China. This time the joint communiqué was more forthright and uncompromising than that of April 1957. It called for an immediate restoration of diplomatic relations, the conclusion of a peace treaty and abolition of the Peace Treaty signed in 1952 between Japan and Nationalist China. This last had been implicit in the party's previous rejection of a 'two Chinas' policy, but not specifically stated in the 1957 communiqué. As it turned out, however, the communiqué issued in 1959 was less important, in terms of its repercussions, than an informal remark allegedly made in Peking by the JSP Secretary-General Asanuma Inejirō, that 'American imperialism is the common enemy of the peoples of Japan and China'. This single sentence was immediately subjected to extravagant approbation by the Chinese and was treated by the Japanese press with equivalent hostility.[25]

The exact circumstances in which the 'Asanuma statement' was made remain obscure, but in any case the Chinese were able to exploit it in such a way that the JSP delegation became committed to a more radical position than it had planned to adopt. According to one source (a member of the equally controversial 1962 JSP delegation to Peking) the cause of the trouble was that the Chinese press quoted Asanuma out of context; what he in fact said was this:

> In so far as it has occupied and equipped with nuclear weapons both Taiwan, which is Chinese soil, and Okinawa, which is Japanese soil, and has turned them into Far Eastern bases, American imperialism must be harmful to, and the common enemy of, the peoples of Japan and China.[26]

The clause beginning 'in so far as' could therefore be taken as a qualification of the 'Asanuma statement' as relayed to the Japanese press. Even if this interpretation is accepted, however, it is a fact that the sentiment expressed was sufficiently radical to cause dissension within the 1959 delegation itself. The following version of what actually happened was given to the writer by a leading member of the delegation.[27] According to this informant, Asanuma's remarks were made in a speech delivered shortly after the delegation arrived. At a later exchange of speeches he again used the same words, but this time other members of the delegation had seen the speech in advance and knew that the offending phrase did not occur in the manuscript. In the opinion of the informant it had been inserted at the last minute at the suggestion of a North Korean official who was a friend of Asanuma. The Chinese side then strongly urged that the phrase be inserted into the joint communiqué, but the members of the delegation after some discussion decided that this was impossible. They conceded, however, that the Peace Treaty between Japan and Nationalist China should be condemned in the joint communiqué in stronger terms than they would themselves have chosen. The delegates refused to insert the 'Asanuma statement' into the joint communiqué primarily because of the current crisis over the offshore islands, in which communist China desired JSP support. A commitment by the party to give even moral support to communist China on this issue might, they felt, put the party in a difficult position if the Chinese were to launch an attack on American personnel.[28] If this version of events is substantially correct it would suggest that the party, while stopping short of capitulation to Chinese demands, had nevertheless shifted its foreign policy well to the left since 1955.

This in fact was only one instance of a general leftward trend that had taken place in the party since reunification. This trend was in part a factional matter.[29] It will be recalled that reunification was promoted by the Suzuki and Kawakami factions—the leading factions of the former Left and Right Socialists respectively. Of these the Suzuki faction attained increasing dominance, securing an increasing number of top party posts into its own hands. Moreover its leader, Suzuki Mosaburō, remained party Chairman until 1960. With strong backing from *Sōhyō* the Suzuki faction was able to dominate the Kawakami faction, its partner in a 'main stream' alliance, especially as the latter was very weakly based in the trade unions. As might have been expected, this tended to upset the delicate balance that had been constructed in 1955. Moreover the results of the Lower House elections in 1958 were disappointing: the party failed to advance as it had in previous elections.[30] Predictably, the factions began to try to pin responsibility for this failure upon each other.

An article by Professor Sakisaka of the *Shakaishugi Kyōkai* became the rallying point for the extreme left. Sakisaka criticized the 1955 reunification agreement for diluting the true revolutionary doctrine according to which the organized mass of workers must be prepared to seize power from the capitalists by force if necessary. He therefore advocated mass action by the working class.[31] The three most left wing factions of the JSP (Wada, Nomizo and Matsumoto) responded favourably to the article, as did the leadership of *Sōhyō*.

The fact that the *Sōhyō* leaders had come to support Sakisaka's doctrinaire views about revolutionary organization was of especial significance. In 1955 effective control of *Sōhyō* passed out of the hands of Takano into those of Ōta Kaoru, who emphasized economic rather than political objectives for the trade union movement. One of Ōta's main aims was to co-ordinate the activities of labour on an industry basis and thus gradually break down the enterprise-union structure of labour organization, which had always served to weaken its bargaining power. Mass campaigns for purely political aims were not really part of his philosophy.

The backing given by *Sōhyō* for the 'Sakisaka Thesis' marked a departure from these principles. The unprecedented size of the mass movement in November 1958 against the Police Duties Bill, which aimed to increase the powers of the police, forced the government to back down and thus demonstrated to the *Sōhyō* leaders how effective a mass movement could be in certain circumstances. The stronger resistance of employers to trade union demands since the advent of the Kishi government was a furthur stimulus to radicalism in *Sōhyō*. Meanwhile the influence of *Sōhyō* over the left wing factions of the JSP had significantly increased since the early 1950s. This was mainly because of the chronic weakness of Socialist organization, which drove the party to seek trade union funds for candidates at elections. A Socialist parliamentary candidate with trade union backing had a far greater chance of being elected than a candidate who had to rely only on the support of the party and his faction.[32] In December 1958 the dominance of *Sōhyō* was aptly demonstrated when the Suzuki faction, despite its almost unchallenged position on the party executive, complied promptly with a *Sōhyō* demand for a more revolutionary approach to the question of achieving power.[33]

In the face of the increasing radicalism of the party's left wing, the Nishio faction began openly to spread its own doctrine of a 'people's party' not entirely dependent on organized labour, and of scrupulous adherence to parliamentary principles.[34] In foreign policy the faction alleged that the party leadership had become virulently pro-communist and anti-American. It called for something more constructive than mere blanket opposition to revision of the Security Treaty, and while not objecting to the principle of 'positive neutrality', maintained that it was being distorted to fit a biased, one-sided view of world affairs. While some on the far left of the party were arguing that neutralism was only possible because communist countries—by definition incapable of aggression themselves—were capable of deterring aggression by capitalist countries, the Nishio faction denied that such a view was in any way implied by neutralism.[35]

The dispute between the Nishio faction and the rest came to a head in October 1959 when, following a censure motion against him, Nishio led his own faction and some members of the Kawakami faction out of the party altogether. Thus in early 1960 the Democratic Socialist Party (DSP) was born. The new party soon adopted a more pro-western view of foreign policy than had the Nishio faction between 1955 and 1959 when, presumably, its stand was affected by the need to compromise. The DSP called on Japan to support the western camp while maintaining wide freedom of action for her own diplomacy.

The leftward drift of the JSP in foreign policy was thus but one indication of a trend to the left in party policy as a whole. Some of Kishi's policy aims (revision of the Security Treaty, strengthening of the Self-Defence Forces, constitutional revision to emasculate the 'pacifist clause', coolness towards Peking) gave rise to mounting left wing resentment, as did some of his domestic policies. This resentment showed itself in more radical forms of anti-government campaigns, such as that against the Police Duties Bill, and later against revision of the Security Treaty.

Apart from this, however, the party's policies were much affected by the internal balance of factions. The unification compromise had been engineered for their mutual benefit by the moderate left and moderate right in circumstances that permitted moderation. From 1958 electoral and organizational stagnation helped to polarize the extreme right and extreme left. The ideological struggle centred on two uncompromising figures—Sakisaka, a Marxist academic of a fundamentalist school, and Nishio, a tough and rather unintellectual ex-trade unionist. The centre factions were therefore forced to commit themselves to one side or the other. Because of its close connections with *Sōhyō* it is not surprising that the Suzuki faction swung from its centre position to an alliance with the far left, after the *Sōhyō* leadership had done likewise. It is more surprising that Asanuma, long associated with the Kawakami faction, should have preserved his alliance with Suzuki by following him along extremist paths which alienated much of the Kawakami faction itself.[36]

Whatever Asanuma's reasons may have been, his action weakened what cohesion the moderate centre might have had in the ensuing crisis over the Security Treaty. The 'Asanuma statement', whatever its original motivation, became symbolic of an extremist anti-Americanism associated with the Suzuki-Asanuma leadership. 'Positive neutrality' as interpreted by the increasingly left wing oriented party leaders was a specifically anti-American weapon, and it was only after the replacement of the Suzuki-Asanuma partnership in 1960 that the way was open for a more moderate form of neutralism.

9

'POSITIVE NEUTRALITY' AND
'STRUCTURAL REFORM'

In any future political history of modern Japan the year 1960 is almost certain to be regarded as a watershed. During May and June a combination of events led to demonstrations of unprecedented size and vociferousness against revision of the Security Treaty. The handling of the crisis by Prime Minister Kishi, and in particular his introduction of police into the Diet in order to cope with Socialist and Communist obstruction, much exacerbated the intensity of feeling against him, although it ensured ratification of the revised Treaty. The crisis made it necessary for Kishi to advise President Eisenhower that the personal safety of the President could not be guaranteed if he visited Japan as scheduled on the day that the treaty was to come into effect. The visit was cancelled and shortly afterwards Kishi was forced to resign by a combination of factions against him in his own Liberal-Democratic Party.

The dynamics of this crisis have been discussed elsewhere,[1] but what is significant for our purposes is its long-term effects. With 1960 as the turning point, a period of comparatively low-tension politics was now to succeed a period when political tensions had been high. Kishi's successor as Prime Minister, Ikeda Hayato, prudently decided to concentrate on economic rather than political goals. Instead of pushing forward with controversial attempts to revise the Constitution and to innovate in foreign policy, he turned to the elaboration of a ten-year plan for the economy, which was currently showing extremely high growth rates. In a more fundamental sense, the 1960 crisis could be considered a turning point in the stabilization of political patterns. It marked the end of an era of search and experimentation with the new political forms introduced during the Occupation, and the beginning of a period of greater regularity and predictability. Two main parties—each of them loose alliances of factions—now faced each other in a confrontation that was fundamentally unequal, but in which each party acted with some sense of the limits beyond which it was undesirable to provoke the other. For the time being the rapid electoral advances of the Socialists in the early 1950s had been halted and the results of one general election differed little from those of the last. Although by 1967 the signs of change were once more proliferating, in the earlier part of the decade the picture was rather one of unexciting stability and thankful withdrawal from the perilous adventures that had culminated in the 1960 crisis.

In the JSP in particular 1960 was seen as a turning point. As we have seen, its domestic and foreign policies had moved steadily to the left since 1955, a course that had once more disastrously split the party. Were the Japanese socialists to continue their militancy in a new climate of government moderation, or were they to step back, reappraise their stand on fundamental issues and perhaps thereby appeal to a wider section of the electorate? As always the clarity of the choice was clouded by the presence of constant factional conflict. This was moreover a time when the long-established factional patterns within the party were undergoing a profound change, corresponding in part to a generational shift in the leadership. For most of the post-war period it had been possible to place the seven or eight factions along an ideological spectrum, from right to left, the nature of which tended to determine to a considerable extent factional alliances and hostilities. On the several occasions when the party had split, it had always been a question either of a left wing alliance confronting a right wing alliance, or a faction at one extreme or the other defying the rest of the party. It was particularly easy to classify the factions according to their respective stands on foreign policy, which ranged from the pro-communism of the extreme left through gradations of neutralism (distinguished by greater and lesser degrees of anti-Americanism) to an anti-communist sympathy with much of the American global position, on the far right. From 1960, however, the factional situation became more fluid, and there was a partial breakdown in the relationship between a faction's ideology and its motivations for alliance with other factions. The controversies over neutralism and related issues show up this trend very clearly.

The anti-Security Treaty demonstrations of May and June 1960 were followed by a restatement of 'positive neutrality' by the JSP in rather more moderate terms. Fighting under the new slogan of 'A government for defence of the Constitution, for democracy and for neutralism', the party repeated most of its previous neutralist aims, such as non-alignment with military blocs, an international guarantee of Japanese security, friendly relations with all countries and total disarmament. It was now careful to stress, however, that neutralism meant independence from the Soviet bloc as much as it meant independence from the United States.[2] By implication the 'Asanuma statement' was rejected: Socialist co-operation with the JCP during the Security Treaty crisis was followed by a reaction against that party and once more the neutralism professed by the Communists was denounced as a sham.[3] Alongside its condemnation of the Security Treaty the JSP now consciously directed some of its fire against the Sino-Soviet Treaty of Friendship signed in 1950.[4]

As an earnest of its intention to develop a truly impartial neutralism, the party now proposed to send delegations not only to the Soviet Union and communist China, but also to a country with which its relations could hardly at the time have been worse, namely the United States. In reply to the Communist criticism of this move the Socialists pointed to President Kennedy's election as heralding a new flexibility in American foreign policy.[5] The plan, however, immediately met some fierce criticism from the party's own left wing, and came to be regarded with more general scepticism once the contours of the Kennedy Administration's foreign policy became known. The Ikeda-Kennedy conference held in June 1961, which served to confirm American-Japanese solidarity under the revised Security Treaty, finally led to the planned delegation being shelved.[6]

The party fulfilled its intention of sending a delegation to the Soviet Union, but this achieved little of significance or controversy. The real touchstone of policy, however, was the proposed delegation to Peking. This would be the third such mission sent by the party since 1955. The second, in 1959, had resulted in the 'Asanuma statement' and had caused a great deal of embarrassment. In the meantime Asanuma had been assassinated by an ultra-rightist fanatic and had acquired the aura of martyrdom. Was the 'Asanuma statement' to be officially reconfirmed, as the Chinese were certain to demand? In January 1962, after repeated delays, a delegation went to Peking led by the party's former Chairman Suzuki Mosaburō, who, it will be recalled, had been closely associated with Asanuma himself between 1955 and 1960. In the event the delegates returned having affixed their seals to a joint communiqué which not only reiterated that American imperialism was the common enemy of the peoples of Japan and China, but also stated that the struggles of both peoples against American imperialism should be intensified.[7]

In view of the efforts that had recently been made within the party to swing its foreign policy back from the left to the centre, we may well ask why this denouement had been allowed to occur. In the first place it should be noted that the delegation did not go along with the Chinese on all points. The two sides failed to agree on the matter of neutralism, and in the joint communiqué expressed their respective positions separately as an 'exchange of views'. The Chinese stated their support for the neutralization of Japan, but specifically interpreted this in the negative sense of an end to Japan's American connection. In this case it would be up to Japan to choose her social system, and China would not force a military alliance upon her. The Japanese Socialists, in contrast, merely declared in terms of enthusiasm that the greatest possible guarantee of peace in Asia would be the conversion of Japan to unarmed neutralism. Moreover, according to one delegate, he and his colleagues found themselves sharply disagreeing with their Chinese hosts, particularly about whether to reaffirm the 'Asanuma statement', but also on the emphasis to be placed on general disarmament and the settling of international disputes by peaceful means. According to this delegate, the talks were nearly broken off on two or three occasions.[8]

Although the delegation was clearly under great pressure from the Chinese side to express support for a militantly anti-American line, it seems that the Chinese were abetted by JSP delegates belonging to a small pro-communist faction known as *Heiwa Dōshikai*. The delegation's membership was more heavily biased in favour of this faction than was warranted by its strength within the party, and was weighted in favour of the left wing group of factions which opposed the current party leadership (this left wing group included Suzuki's own faction) by a proportion of two to one. Judging from the record of ideological conflict between Suzuki's faction and the extreme left now represented by the *Heiwa Dōshikai*, he can scarcely have been pleased with the pressure evidently placed upon him by the latter. As leader of the delegation, indeed, he found himself in an embarrassing position. Upon his return, he gave a somewhat tortured explanation of the reasoning behind the joint communiqué, arguing along true *Rōnō-ha* lines that while China was confronted with only one external enemy, namely American imperialism, Japan was faced not only with this but also with the dangers from her own monopoly capital. Nevertheless, he maintained, the Japanese people also were 'suffocated' by American imperialism. The posthumous prestige of Asanuma had also, according to his account, been an important factor in the minds of the delegates.[9]

Few events illustrate better the tensions which had been aroused in the party by the 'Asanuma statement' than the aftermath of the 1962 Japanese Socialist delegation to China. In August of the same year after the House of Councillors elections—always a deterrent to open factional strife—were safely over, Suzuki formally retracted his reaffirmation of the 'Asanuma statement', stating that he had been forced to lend his name to the joint communiqué by members of the delegation affiliated with the *Heiwa Dōshikai*.[10] The details of motivation involved remain obscure, but Suzuki probably wanted to assert his faction's ideological independence. The *Heiwa Dōshikai* was pro-communist in a much more fundamental sense than any other faction in the party, and therefore tactical alliances between it and other factions tended to encounter serious problems of ideology and outlook.

The problem of a small but more or less overtly pro-communist faction within the JSP leads us on to the important question of inter-party relations between the JSP and the JCP. Despite the similarity of some of their aims, their views on aspects of foreign policy were at this stage increasingly divergent. Nowhere did this divergence become more evident than in the peace movement, one of the most important mass organizations from the point of view of both parties. The movement gave to the JSP a series of opportunities to express and develop, in the face of determined communist opposition, its own policies of neutralism. As we shall see, it was to face considerable difficulties in maintaining the integrity of these policies in a changing world.

Gensuikyō, originally a non-partisan organization, had come to acquire a more and more left wing character. In protest against this trend a small splinter group, associated with the DSP, broke away in 1961. This left wing trend in fact meant increasing control by the JCP. At the *Gensuikyō* Congress held in Hiroshima in August 1961, socialists and communists clashed over the question of nuclear testing. The final resolution of the Congress declared that the government which first broke the current nuclear test moratorium should be censured as the enemy of peace and humanity. It went on, however, to criticize American 'imperialism' as the main cause of international tension.[11] The JSP, *Sōhyō* and two other organizations affiliated with *Gensuikyō* issued a dissenting resolution attacking the *Gensuikyō* executive for its autocratic methods and extreme objectives.[12] At the same time the official JSP newspaper criticized the leaders of the anti-nuclear movement for minimizing the dangers of an all out east-west conflict and the considerable responsibility of the Soviet Union for the current hardening of international tension.[13]

Shortly afterwards the Soviet Union unilaterally broke the nuclear test moratorium. Nothing could have been more exactly calculated to exacerbate differences between the JSP and the JCP. The JCP was quick to support the Soviet action, declaring that 'since the Soviet Union is a peace force, nuclear tests are a natural defensive measure'. Rejecting Socialist criticism that the new round of testing would raise global levels of radioactivity

still higher, the party reiterated that the main danger to world
peace sprang not from nuclear fallout but from the American
imperialists.[14]

This view, in turn, called forth some trenchant criticism
from a new and important JSP leader, Eda Saburō (of whom
more will be said later). Attacking the opinion, emanating from
the JCP, that Soviet tests were in some way beneficial to
humanity while those of the United States were not, he called
for a peace movement based on 'positive neutrality':

> No matter which side actually starts a world war, it will
> result in the death of humanity. Fallout falls on both sides
> alike. Granted that the power of imperialism is limited by
> the existence of the Soviet Union, no peace movement can
> survive in the belief that peace is preserved by a balance of
> power . . . On the contrary, we wish to abolish the balance
> of terror, ban nuclear weapons and achieve total disarmament,
> thus rooting out the very essence of power politics.[15]

Such an attitude placed the *Heiwa Dōshikai* in a difficult
position. It could not defy the current set of party leaders to the
extent of openly supporting the communist line on nuclear
testing. Instead it took the median standpoint, that although
American and Soviet tests were 'qualitatively different', the
dangers from nuclear fallout made it important to try to stop
both.[16]

Gensuikyō, torn between socialists and communists, despera-
tely attempted to compromise by condemning the Soviet action
but at the same time condoning it by reference to the recent
series of French tests and alleged provocation by NATO.[17] A
year later not even such a papering of the cracks was possible.
At the Hiroshima Congress of August 1962 the Socialists spared
no means, including physical force, to gain control of the communist-dominated platform, and when they failed in this
endeavour they walked out of the Congress. Added point was
given to the controversy by the coincidence of another series of
Soviet tests.[18] In 1963 left wing politics in Japan had already
begun to be affected by the Sino-Soviet dispute which had flared
in the early months of that year. *Gensuikyō* held its annual
Congress in August, shortly after the United States, the Soviet

Union, Great Britain and other countries had signed a partial nuclear test-ban treaty, denounced forthwith by communist China. The Socialists, consistent with their opposition to nuclear testing by any power whatever, welcomed the treaty, while the Communists, already on the road to a pro-Peking alignment, championed the Chinese rejection. In these circumstances the anti-nuclear movement finally and apparently irrevocably split.[19]

The issue of nuclear testing and, finally, the Sino-Soviet dispute served, by the measure of disagreement with the JCP, to confirm the JSP leaders in their policy of 'positive neutrality'. In recent years the party's most left wing and intransigent pronouncements on foreign policy had borne the imprint of pressure from Peking. The Socialists had consistently tried to improve Japan's relations with communist China, and on occasion this had placed weapons in the hands of extreme leftists within the JSP. The Sino-Soviet dispute, however, tended to weaken for the time being any Chinese capacity to influence the party. China's pronouncements on the inevitability of war with 'imperialism', her border conflict with India in late 1962, her declared aim of 'going nuclear' and the denunciation of the test-ban treaty, alienated many socialists in Japan. Relations between the JSP and communist China became increasingly cool, although the *Heiwa Dōshikai* had leanings in the Chinese direction. Later events were to show, however, that Chinese influence upon the party was not necessarily at an end.

So far we have looked at Socialist foreign policy from 1960 without reference to a momentous power struggle which had been developing within the party. This in itself, quite apart from external issues, was an important determinant of foreign policy and must now be woven into the picture.

The power struggle concerned the appearance in the party of a new ideological approach to revolution and the achievement of socialism, called Structural Reform. This theory, which derived from Togliatti's Italian Communist Party, was first discussed in 1958 by a small group in the Suzuki faction. It did not, however, become an issue in the dispute then raging between the Nishio faction and the factions of the left. A radical change in ideology was not to be expected under the Suzuki-Asanuma leadership, which had dominated the party since

1955. In late 1960, however, after a period of discussion by the executive but without general debate, Structural Reform was introduced as official party policy. Its implications were that a socialist revolution could take place as the end-product of a process of slow and steady pressure by trade unions and the JSP for the achievement of better wages and conditions. The process would in the end alter the balance of power between labour and capital to such an extent that revolution could be achieved without the cataclysm thought inevitable hitherto by many left wing socialists.[20] These socialists had often argued that *ad hoc* reform was basically futile since it would tend to mitigate the evils that must in the end result in revolution.[21] Structural Reform did not dispense with the final revolutionary aim, but said that labour was now potentially strong enough to get there by a more or less gradual progression.

In some ways the content of the theory was less important than the personalities and fortunes of the men who sponsored it, and the nature of the backing they received. It is necessary to recall that 1960 was a year of crisis for the JSP, as for Japanese politics in general. There were several reasons for this. The party's failure to advance electorally had caused a crisis of confidence which was compounded by the defection of a substantial part of the right wing.[22] The emphasis of the new Ikeda cabinet upon economic growth and moderate politics put the JSP in need of a programme that could compete on even terms. Also the party's recent experience of struggles not confined to the Diet, particularly those against the Police Duties Bill and against revision of the Security Treaty, as well as a prolonged and bitter strike at the Miike coal field, while indicating the potentialities of such direct action, suggested also that a total refusal to compromise could be harmful to the party's interests.

Apart from these general factors, however, the party was undergoing profound changes in the composition and balance of its leadership. Since 1955 the JSP had been dominated by the Suzuki and Kawakami factions. When the Nishio faction defected, it was followed by a considerable part of the Kawakami faction, leaving the Suzuki faction in much the most powerful position in the party.

Prior to the party Congress of March 1960 Suzuki himself resigned from the Chairmanship, supporting Asanuma as his successor. The remnant of the Kawakami faction put up its leader Kawakami as a rival candidate, and the party presented the most unusual spectacle of an election for high office fought between men who were officially members of the same faction. Kawakami received a considerable number of votes from delegates anxious to stem further defections from his faction into the ranks of the DSP, which would have meant a further weakening of the JSP.[23] In the event Asanuma narrowly defeated Kawakami by 228 votes to 209, and a hitherto little-known figure from the Suzuki faction, Eda Saburō, was elected Secretary-General. Later in the year Asanuma was killed by a youth associated with an ultra-rightist lunatic-fringe organization, and Eda stepped into his shoes as acting Chairman.

Eda's meteoric rise to power was essentially the product of chance circumstances. Suzuki's presumptive successor was an old fashioned and extremely doctrinaire politician named Sasaki Kōzō, principally known hitherto for his adeptness at behind-the-scenes factional manipulation. Although Sasaki was later able to turn his lack of oratorical ability to some advantage by appealing to the ordinary voter as an unsophisticated 'man of the people' (he spoke with a strong rustic accent which sounded uncouth in metropolitan Tokyo) in 1960 this could hardly have been predicted. Nevertheless, he was known to be the 'strong man' of the faction, and his reasons for allowing the faction to sponsor Eda for high office instead of himself are not known. It may, of course, have been the case that he was merely following the long-established Japanese tradition of the strong-man who finds it more desirable to exercise power covertly, through a figurehead, than to assume the formal trappings of power himself. If so, Sasaki was sorely disappointed, for Eda as it turned out did not remain content with his position as Sasaki's stooge. With a brilliance of silver-tongued oratory matched only by the silvery-greyness of his hair, Eda rapidly became known through his frequent television appearances as the 'lady-killer'. His successes against the new Prime Minister in a series of television debates preceding the Lower House general elections of November 1960 greatly added to his reputation and personal popularity with the Japanese public (although they did not, it seems, greatly add to the socialist vote). Unlike Sasaki, Eda was prepared to be ideologically flexible and to appreciate the opportunities presented by factional imbalance and the demise of much of the old-style party leadership for a radical restructuring of the whole party under his own leadership. It is principally as a doctrinal weapon in this endeavour that his introduction of the theory of Structural Reform towards the end of 1960 must be understood.

There is no denying that Eda was personally ambitious, or that Structural Reform brought a 'wind of change' into a party that was in danger of bogging down in increasingly stale and irrelevant controversy. That he was himself free from backstage manipulation is, however, much more doubtful. The fact that he had refused to toe Sasaki's line did not mean that he could avoid being the servant of any other interest in the party. He did not, it is true, have factional backing in the normal sense. During 1961 he and one or two adherents (notably his close colleague Narita Tomomi) dissociated themselves from the Sasaki (formerly Suzuki) faction, and they were henceforth dubbed the 'Eda faction'.[24] It was not, however, for some considerable time that this 'faction' acquired significant parliamentary strength.

Eda's backers belonged to two closely related groups. The first was a small band of ex-Communist theorists that had joined the JSP after their faction championing Togliatti's theories was expelled from the JCP in 1961. Some of these men became influential exponents of Structural Reform, and their views were often clearly reflected in Eda's speeches. For a time the extent of their influence even brought the new theory under suspicion by some in the party as a communist import, despite the moderation of its tone relative to the prevailing *Rōnō-ha* doctrines.[25] Much more important was the support which Eda received from paid party officials contesting the hitherto paramount influence of factions composed mainly of parliamentarians. At the party Congress of 1958 the parliamentarians received a considerable setback owing to a change in the rules governing the composition of national party congresses. Previously it had been obligatory for each local branch of the party to elect its local Socialist Diet member as a delegate to the congress. Now, however, they could elect delegates of their choice without this restriction.[26] This change implied that the strength of a faction in the Diet did not necessarily mean that it could muster an equivalent strength at a party congress, and the power of party officials and local branches increased accordingly.

The introduction of Structural Reform resulted, after an initial period of manoeuvring, in a new balance of party factions. It was immediately opposed by a left wing coalition, composed of the *Heiwa Dōshikai*, the *Shakaishugi Kyōkai* (led by Professor Sakisaka), the small and insignificant Nomizo faction, the top leadership of *Sōhyō* (notably Ōta), and most important, the Sasaki faction.[27] This was a coalition very similar to the left wing alliances that had opposed unification in 1955 and had forced Nishio out of the party in 1959. It concealed the old ideological squabble between the pro-communist *Heiwa Dōshikai*, which wanted to give precedence to a 'revolution of national liberation' and the rest, which mostly attacked it from a *Rōnō-ha* standpoint.

Apart from his direct backers, Eda came to receive support from two parliamentary factions, those of Kawakami and Wada. The Kawakami faction was in a weak position since it had split. In return for supporting Eda for Secretary-General, Kawakami's election as party Chairman was now assured, although he was generally regarded as little more than a figurehead in this position. Since Structural Reform was opposed by a left wing coalition, it is scarcely surprising if the Kawakami faction—sole remnant of the traditional right wing—should have given it a measure of support.

The role played, in contrast, by the Wada faction showed how complex the relationship between factional manoeuvre and ideology had become. Wada, one of the very few Socialist leaders who had had a career in the bureaucracy, was Minister of Agriculture for a short period early in the Occupation before joining the JSP and committing himself to its semi-Marxist wing. His faction contained a nucleus of like-minded ex-bureaucrats (notably Katsumata Seiichi, Sata Tadataka and Wada himself) who had between them controlled the party's Foreign Policy Bureau over a long period. During the late 1950s its rivalry with the Suzuki faction had led it to seek allies to the left of that faction, giving it a reputation for extremism. Now, however, it was faced by a new balance of forces and opportunities that it had been previously denied. When Structural Reform was first introduced the Wada faction was thought likely to commit itself to the anti-Eda camp, and a bitter personal rivalry between Eda and Wada was much discussed.[28] This, however, was smoothed over, and by late 1961 the Wada faction had joined the 'main-stream' factional alliance in support of Structural Reform.[29]

What effects did this new power structure have upon attitudes to 'positive neutrality'?

One striking feature of the situation was that ultra-left wing interpretations of (or deviations from) neutralism on the part of the Sasaki faction (for instance Suzuki's reaffirmation of the Asanuma statement in January 1962) were dictated to a large extent by its factional alliance with the small but vociferous *Heiwa Dōshikai*. The ideological differences between the two factions, though to a non-Marxist observer they might seem slight, had existed for many years and were bitterly felt. Nevertheless the needs of a power struggle precipitated by the upstart group of Structural Reformers were sufficient to push the Sasaki faction into an extremism over foreign policy that from an ideological point of view could be dubbed 'unprincipled'. The same sort of thing had happened in the late 1950s in the dispute with Nishio, suggesting that the faction found it hard to resist left wing pressure in any struggle with the right. This seems rather surprising in view of the faction's grass-roots strength among the party rank and file.

If we examine the attitudes to neutralism exhibited by the new 'leadership' group of factions, a not dissimilar picture emerges, with the factional power struggle assuming primacy over ideological and policy concerns. There were of course many instances of a like opportunism in the earlier post-war years, but a careful comparison of the two periods reveals in the first half of the 1960s a diminished preoccupation with ideological consistency. It may be suggested that the JSP was in the process of outgrowing its origins and was becoming, in its internal behaviour at least, rather more like other Japanese political parties.

Now neutralism was certainly a concept whose ambiguity led to divergences in interpretation. For a party strongly influenced by Marxism, it was not always easy to be 'neutral' between the rival camps of 'socialism' and 'capitalism'. Nor was the dilemma made any easier by the fact that the government's foreign policy was pro-American, and by the strength of Japan's defence and trade links with the United States which in socialist eyes prejudiced Japan's independence. The very ambiguity, however, of neutralism as a concept pointed to a means of reconciling it with the party's basic *Weltanschauung*. The ambiguity lay in the difference between ideological and political neutralism. Neutralism in the sense of having (or expressing) no preference between two rival concepts of how to organize society, differed from neutralism in the sense of refusing to enter into military alliances with the nations constituting either of the rival blocs, even though the rivalry of these blocs derived in part at least from their contrasting ideologies. Since a refusal to enter into military alliances with either bloc meant in practice an end to the Security Treaty with the United States, the ideological anti-Americanism of many socialists was satisfied by a purely political neutralism. This is not to imply, however, that neutralism was not taken seriously within the party. Indeed it was the subject of much disputation.

The anti-leadership factions, as we have seen, tended to interpret neutralism mainly in anti-American terms, and generally speaking did not produce any sophisticated interpretation of neutralism as such. The main foreign policy clashes within the party came between this kind of view and the various readings of neutralism that emanated from the 'leadership' factions.

Although differences of interpretation among the 'leadership' factions themselves were of secondary importance in the power struggle, they raise interesting issues concerning the substance of a neutralist policy as argued by socialist politicians. In particular, the views of Eda and his immediate followers contrasted at this period with those expressed by leading members of the Wada and Kawakami factions.

The expositions of neutralism made by Eda owed much to a journalist, Satō Noboru, who joined the JSP after seceding from the JCP in July 1961 together with a group supporting Structural Reform. So far as foreign policy was concerned, Satō came to be regarded as the 'brains' behind Eda, and indeed his brand of neutralism, expressed in an article written in October 1961,[30] was closely followed by Eda in subsequent foreign policy pronouncements.[31]

Satō argued that it was necessary to distinguish three aspects of the east-west struggle: first, the difference between the American and Soviet systems, defined respectively as 'imperialist' and 'socialist'; second, a difference at the level of policy—between the peaceful policies of socialism and the warlike policies of capitalism. He argued that between these two sets of alternatives, no socialist could remain neutral. The east-west struggle was, however, also an armed struggle between military blocs, and pregnant with the possibility of nuclear war. At this third level, he insisted, neutralism was essential in order to save the human race from nuclear destruction. It was, moreover, the 'peace policies' and the overall strength of the Soviet camp which rendered neutralism both practicable and desirable for a nation like Japan. Interestingly enough he criticized neutralism as practised by Yugoslavia, on the grounds that that country was by geography and history part of the Soviet bloc, and should not, therefore, neglect her special duties of solidarity and collective defence with her socialist comrades.

The somewhat paradoxical message of this article, that in order to get rid of the cold war between rival military blocs, a country not in the front line should be neutral, but that this neutralism was made possible only by the relative strength and by the 'peace policies' of the Soviet bloc, did not prove acceptable to all elements among the 'leadership' factions.

In particular Wada Hiroo, important both as faction leader and current Chairman of the party's Foreign Policy Bureau, gave expression to a far less Soviet-oriented neutralism.[32] He agreed with Satō that the main justification for neutralism was that neutralist nations could help prevent a 'hot' war between east and west, but he made no use of Satō's argument against ideological neutralism. On the contrary, he thought the peace-potential of non-aligned nations bore no relation to the type of political system that each might possess. The 1961 Belgrade Conference of Non-Aligned Nations had demonstrated that countries owing allegiance to neither bloc now had more sense of their own unity and strength in world politics than they had a decade earlier. Even Takano's 'peace forces' argument, put forward in 1953, had a certain rationale at that time because the concept of neutralist nations as guarantors of peace was then only in an embryo stage.

It followed from Wada's approach that both 'capitalist' and 'socialist' nations could successfully mediate in international disputes threatening world peace. Thus he instanced the potential 'third force' role of Britain and Western Europe, while to make his point completely clear he praised the mediation of the United States in the West Irian dispute of 1962.[33]

The discrepancy in these two approaches was shown up during the formulation of the party's official Action Policy for 1962. In November 1961 Eda issued a 'political report' in which he stated that American 'imperialism' was a 'war force' while the Soviet Union was a 'peace force'. Indeed the argument of the report was virtually identical with that of the article by Satō Noboru. Subsequently some parts of the report—notably a phrase ascribing the chief cause of east-west tension to American 'imperialism'—were amended at the insistence of other members of the executive.[34] According to press reports, Wada was chiefly instrumental in obtaining these amendments.[35] Wada also apparently objected to the report's implication that the world balance of power was shifting decisively in favour of the communist bloc, and that as a partial consequence of this the United States was seeking to promote Japanese expansionism in Korea and Taiwan, so as to provide itself with a bastion against further communist encroachments upon its sphere of interests.

It should thus be fairly evident that although 'positive neutrality' remained the official basis for the party's foreign policy, there was a persistent tendency to pull it 'left of centre'. In a sense this was scarcely surprising, since the secession of the whole of the Nishio faction and a substantial part of the Kawakami faction had robbed the JSP of most of its traditional right wing. All these factional manoeuvres that have been described were directed towards the establishment of a new factional balance to replace that which had been shattered in 1959–60. By early 1963 a new and fairly stable balance had been achieved. In the process, however, some of the traditional ideological divisions between the factions had become blurred. The Sasaki faction seemed to have fallen under the strong influence of its traditional ideological rival, the *Heiwa Dōshikai*. The Wada faction, at least on foreign policy, had moved from the left of the party to the right. The remnant of the Kawakami faction, alone, had undergone little change of attitude. The new Structural Reform group, though obviously swinging to the right in domestic policy, remained left of centre so far as its exposition of neutralism was concerned.

It is difficult to escape the conclusion that the JSP over this period was becoming, at least in its behaviour, more like other Japanese political parties, notably the Liberal-Democrats. In other words, pure factional advantage was becoming rather more important, while intra-party quarrels with a mainly ideological motivation were receding into the background. This is not to say that the JSP was already on the road to becoming a party of moderate and pragmatic policies, as had happened with social-democratic parties in Western Europe, although towards the end of 1962 there was a time when it seemed this might perhaps be happening. The radicalism of the trade union-based party rank and file, as well as the continued appeal of radicalism to a substantial portion of the electorate, ensured the indefinite postponement of the strong moderate and pragmatic socialist party hoped for by some Japanese intellectuals and many foreign observers. Nevertheless, in the party's internal behaviour, as distinct from its official pronouncements, there is ample evidence to suggest that 'ideology for ideology's sake' was an attitude of the past. In foreign policy this was coming to mean that views were formulated and declarations made more from consideration of factional manoeuvres and to some extent electoral appeal, than because of innate conviction. There remained, indeed, a certain gap between the continuing ideological flavour of the Action Policies endorsed by successive congresses, or the statements issued by the Central Executive

Committee, and the increasingly pragmatic context in which these declarations were applied. If this did not result in a 'balanced' neutralism, it was because the more successful party leaders judged, rightly or wrongly, that such a policy did not have the potential appeal of a more direct anti-Americanism.

10

NEUTRALIST ECLIPSE?

The hopes for more moderate and flexible policies aroused by Eda's ascendancy were soon to be dashed. In May 1965 his chief rival Sasaki was elected party Chairman and proceeded to lead the party along much more extreme and intransigent paths. The most dramatic change was in the Socialist attitude to China. Late in 1966 at a time when China had lost most of her foreign allies, and when internally she was beset by the upheavals of the Cultural Revolution, Sasaki was quoted as saying to a meeting of his faction that: 'However bad relations may become between China and the Soviet Union, and between the Japanese Communist Party and the Chinese Communist Party, the JSP must continue to deepen its friendly relations with China'.[1]

The reference to the JCP was particularly significant. Perhaps the most astonishing reversal of left wing politics in Japan in recent years has occurred in the positions taken respectively by Socialists and Communists over attitudes to China. Towards the end of 1964 the JSP, under the leadership of the moderates, was obviously backing the Soviet Union against China, while the JCP was entering a period of close alignment with Peking. In contrast, at the beginning of 1967, the JCP had broken with the Chinese, who were subjecting the party to unparalleled abuse, while the JSP, now led by its left wing, was going out of its way to excuse and praise developments in China.

The question was complicated by controversies over the anti-nuclear weapons movement. As we have seen, the 1963 split of *Gensuikyō* into Socialist and Communist controlled splinter groups took place essentially because the Socialists opposed all nuclear testing, while the Chinese, backed by the JCP, made no secret of their nuclear weapons programme. The above-mentioned reversal of roles made nonsense of these positions and further served to disorganize the anti-nuclear weapons movement.

The course taken by the JSP under Sasaki raises two main questions: first, and most obviously, why did the party go in this new direction, which to an outsider might seem damaging to its ultimate prospects? And second, how complete and genuine was the party's commitment to its new line? Did it mean, for instance, that it had finally and irrevocably shed its nuclear pacifism and its neutralist approach to world affairs in favour of an intransigent anti-Americanism based on Chinese foreign policy?

The answers to both of these questions are complicated, but in reflecting upon the former it becomes evident that two factors were of crucial importance. One was simply the failure of Eda's leadership bid to maintain its momentum in the face of Sasaki's relentless factional organization. The other, however, which not only worked to Eda's disadvantage but also probably made a good deal of difference to Sasaki's way of thinking about foreign policy, was the worsening international environment associated with the war in Vietnam and the split in the communist camp. Bad relations between Moscow and Peking have created quite intractable problems for the JSP, much of whose foreign policy had been premised on the harmony of these two ideological centres. The reaction of Sasaki and his supporters to the Vietnam war was to blame American 'imperialism' as the main cause of Chinese and North Vietnamese intransigence. They justified the Chinese nuclear programme as a natural and legitimate defensive measure against the threat presented by the United States, and claimed that any 'internal contradictions' that there might be in contemporary China should not be allowed to divert attention from American global policies, which were the principal danger to peace in Asia.[2]

Can one then say that the party was fully committed to the new line and that its neutralism and pacifism had been finally replaced by 'Chinese' policies? There are a number of reasons for thinking that this was not so. Neither was Sasaki without opposition in the party, nor, it seems, was his commitment to these policies unequivocal. Factionalism, as usual, played a large part.

Let us therefore examine the stages whereby the moderate factions lost control of the party to its left wing, and then analyse the record of the current leadership.

The downward turn of Eda's fortunes must be dated from the so-called 'vision' controversy of late 1962. In August of that year Eda outlined to a provincial audience a 'vision' of a future socialist society based on the high living standards of the United States, Soviet levels of social security, British parliamentary democracy, and the Japanese 'peace' Constitution.[3] Curiously enough the eclecticism of this concept was not entirely new to the party, since in 1953 Takano Minoru (whose extreme left wing views were noted earlier) had announced something quite similar.[4] In 1962, however, the left chose roundly to condemn the 'vision' as a revisionist heresy. In terms of recent party history there was some truth in this assertion, since Eda now echoed Nishio in calling for policies that would appeal to broad sections of the community and not solely to organized labour.

At the party Congress held in November of the same year, Eda had to face what was in effect a resolution of no confidence in his recent conduct and pronouncements as Secretary-General. The resolution was carried by a small margin and Eda chose to resign from his position. The reasons for this defeat are perplexing, especially in view of the vote, two days later, to elect Eda's successor. On that occasion the left wing candidate was easily defeated by Narita Tomomi, Eda's closest associate in the Structural Reform faction, while Eda himself was elected to a lesser party post by a handsome margin.[5] In all probability the initial vote reflected superior organization by the left wing. The unpredictability of congress voting since the rules were changed in 1958 has already been discussed.

The struggle for power between the Structural Reform coalition and the group centred on the Sasaki faction continued as before, although Narita, as Secretary-General, proved more of a tactician and less of an innovator than Eda. The high point of conflict between the two sides came during 1964, when Sasaki's supporters withdrew from all executive positions in the party and proclaimed themselves an 'intra-party opposition'. Towards the end of the year they were pacified by the device of creating two Vice-Chairmanships in addition to the top posts of Chairman and Secretary-General. It was planned that these new positions should be filled by Sasaki and Wada respectively. This arrangement won the approval of the party Congress held in December 1964, which once more returned Kawakami as Chairman and Narita as Secretary-General. The Sasaki 'opposition', however, managed to capture a clear majority of junior executive posts, thus considerably weakening the control over party affairs hitherto exercised by the Structural Reform coalition.

At this point Narita was thrust into the role of mediator between the warring factions. It seems that he interpreted this role in such a way that it brought him into increasing identification with the Sasaki faction itself. His first chance to mediate occurred in the early months of 1965, when the ageing Kawakami expressed his desire to be relieved of the Chairmanship because of ill-health. (Kawakami died later in the year.) Narita's instinct was to avoid having to choose a new Chairman so soon after the extreme manifestations of factional strife in 1964 had been overcome. National elections for the House of Councillors were shortly due to take place and a number of provincial party secretaries strongly urged Narita not to leave the party leaderless with these elections in the offing. Consequently, in May 1965 a special Congress was held to choose a new Chairman, and after a complicated series of factional manoeuvres,[6] Sasaki was elected unopposed.

Thus Eda finally lost to his opponent the precarious control he had once established over the party. In a sense this represented the triumph of traditional methods of factional organization over an attempt to reshape the party structure. Eventually Eda himself was forced to further his ends by the time-honoured technique of organizing a substantial faction based on Diet members. In so doing he consolidated his position as head of the moderate wing of the party and so made his political comeback seem a definite (but yet to be realized) possibility. At the same time, however, the reforming zeal initially associated with Structural Reform gradually ran down, until the political behaviour of its supporters came to differ little from that of its opponents.

The May 1965 Congress also marked the beginning of the Sasaki-Narita duumvirate which lasted until August 1967. These two leaders were confirmed in office by the regular Congress of January 1966 (though by a very narrow margin) and, with a rather wider margin, by the regular Congress of December 1966. Over this period the party was led in a way reminiscent of the Suzuki-Asanuma leadership of 1955-60. Particularly striking was the parallel between Narita and Asanuma. Both began as leaders of moderate factions and both, once they found themselves in harness with left wing leaders whose influence their election had been intended to balance, swung far to the left themselves. Whatever the individual factors involved in these two cases, their remarkable similarity suggests what is confirmed in other ways, namely that in periods of international tension affecting Japan the pressures on party leaders to conform to a militant left wing pattern on foreign policy has tended to be notably stronger than countervailing pressures of moderation. Furthermore, the defection of the Nishio faction means that the left wing is now balanced with less determination than it was in the party crisis of 1958-60 which led to that defection. The 'neo-right wing' has too much in common ideologically with the left to provide so effective an opposition.

The Asanuma-Narita parallel is particularly interesting since their respective cases both occurred in periods when American policies were regarded by the party with particular hostility. On the first occasion the cause was revision of the Security Treaty, and on the second the bombing of North Vietnam. Moreover, in both cases the party regarded the Japanese Prime Minister of the day (Kishi and Satō respectively) as particularly reactionary and pro-American.

The Vietnam war, and especially the American bombing of the North, have undoubtedly helped to make total hostility to the United States a dominant attitude within the party, rather than the minority view it was up to 1965. Significantly, the more moderate views on foreign policy have thrived in the party at times of comparative relaxation of tensions in Asia. Thus the success of the Structural Reform coalition coincided with a much discussed trend towards peaceful co-existence between the United States and the Soviet Union. Although even the Viet-

nam war has failed entirely to arrest this improvement in relations between the two super-powers, the now heightened confrontation between America and China has overshadowed this
fact in the eyes of many JSP members. Thus anti-Americanism,
always a strong force in the party, has once more tended to
swamp more moderate neutralist views.

The recent thinking of both sides is seen in a published
discussion between a member of the party's moderate wing and
one of the more extreme of Sasaki supporters. The moderate
played down the danger of escalation in the Vietnam war and
discussed ways and means whereby the JSP could promote
peace talks. The Sasaki man, on the other hand, put forward a
kind of 'domino' theory in reverse, namely that a respite in
Vietnam could only be bought at the price of encouraging
American 'imperialism' to create trouble in other parts of Asia,
such as Korea and Cambodia. The moral for the JSP was that
it should devote all its energies to fighting against the Japan-
United States Security Treaty and the American military
presence in Okinawa, seen together as the lynch-pin of American
aggression in Asia.[7]

How completely were Sasaki and his followers indeed committed to such views as these? Much in the record of his leadership suggested that the party was now closely aligned with communist China and communist Chinese foreign policies. Yet on
closer examination it appears that the commitment was not
total. Eda accused Sasaki of 'following uncritically the foreign
policy of other countries, and mouthing a specious radicalism'.[8]
This statement was of course a piece of factional polemics, but
the suggestion that the radicalism was specious, that, as Eda
continued, Sasaki had made the party 'left wing in foreign
policy but right wing in domestic policy', is worth noting.

Many of Sasaki's pronouncements after he was first elected
Chairman were fiercely anti-American and pro-Chinese. His
inaugural speech in May 1965 set the tone. In it he made
a bitter attack upon American policy in Vietnam and the
Japanese government of Satō Eisaku for supporting it. The British
Labour government's position on Vietnam was 'shameful'. He
reiterated the 1959 'Asanuma statement' but with the extra
gloss that American imperialism was now the enemy not only

of the peoples of Japan and China, but also of the whole of mankind.[9] There is no doubt that this and similar tirades at the time reflected the widespread revulsion among Japanese progressives against American bombing of North Vietnam, which had just begun. Here was 'American imperialism' acting in Vietnam as the JSP had so frequently insisted it would act against 'national liberation movements' and their supporters in Asia.

At the annual Congress of the JSP held in January 1966, Sasaki and Eda met in open conflict. The prize for which they fought was now the post of party Chairman. The terrain over which they chose to fight was foreign policy. Sasaki ranged over the field of national liberation movements, China's worsening relations with the United States, and the war in Vietnam, and held that American 'imperialism' was responsible by its aggressive policies for the current crisis in Asia. Eda attacked him for ignoring the party's traditional policy of peaceful coexistence, non-alignment and neutralism, and proclaiming instead an unadulterated anti-imperialism. Vietnam, in Eda's opinion, should be regarded not as 'a basic contradiction in the world situation' but as 'a local contradiction' in the process of polycentrism which had been taking place in recent years.[10]

Sasaki apparently took a more moderate line at the Congress itself than in the committee charged with drafting the Action Policy before the Congress. In committee Sasaki is believed to have said that the Vietnam war was an inevitable stage in the transition from capitalism to socialism, and that it would evolve into a third world war.[11] The expectation that Japan could avoid the consequences of such a war was fanciful, and indeed it was the only thing that could bring about a Socialist government in Japan by 1970. At the Congress, however, Sasaki was quoted as reaffirming the party's opposition to nuclear testing by any country (thus presumably including China), as denying that the JSP no longer officially supported the partial nuclear test-ban treaty and as dissociating himself from Chinese policies.[12]

These apparent inconsistencies perhaps smack merely of the contingencies of factional manoeuvre. Behind them appeared to lie a consistency of purpose—to place the JSP within the Chinese orbit. Yet if this is correct, Sasaki would seem to have pursued a curiously indirect route to achieve his goal. One wonders whether China was not being used by Sasaki rather as it is sometimes alleged China uses the JSP.

Some light may be thrown on this puzzle if we trace how the party under his leadership dealt with three perennial problems: relations with the JCP, control over the anti-nuclear weapons movement and relations with communist China herself.

The question of 'joint struggles' between the JSP and the JCP has long been a sensitive subject within the JSP. The 1959–60 campaign against revision of the Security Treaty resulted in some degree of co-operation between the two parties, formalized in an organization called *Ampo Kyōtō (Ampo Hantai, Heiwa to Minshushugi wo Mamoru Kokumin Kaigi)* (People's Congress to Oppose the Security Treaty and to Defend Peace and Democracy). This body, however, did not function between 1960 and 1964. In 1964 the JCP proposed reviving it in order to co-ordinate demonstrations against the presence in Japanese ports of American nuclear-powered submarines. Negotiations, however, broke down, partly because of opposition from *Sōhyō*.

In 1965, however, after Sasaki had become Chairman, the JCP once more revived its proposal, this time in order to co-ordinate struggles against ratification of the treaty between Japan and South Korea. Both parties opposed this treaty on various grounds, the JSP maintaining that it would merely enable Japanese capital to help the Americans bolster up a reactionary dictatorship in Seoul, and postpone the day when the reunification and neutralization of Korea could be achieved. In response to the JCP proposal Sasaki proposed that the two parties should agree to co-ordinate their demonstrations but without any formal co-ordinating body. Although at first there was some resistance to this proposal from *Sōhyō* leaders, several such 'joint struggles' were in fact held while the Diet debated ratification of the treaty.

This, however, did not represent such a break with previous policy as it might seem. Sasaki did not accept the proposals of the Communist side, which were far more ambitious than anything actually accomplished. Moreover, there were a number of precedents at the local level for the sort of co-operation that Sasaki had proposed.

If, however, Sasaki wanted to co-operate with the JCP in a united front aligned with China, he was disappointed by events in the JCP itself. The Japanese Communists were, in early 1966, one of the last communist parties in the world to remain aligned with Peking. In March of that year, however, a delegation headed by the party's Secretary-General, Miyamoto Kenji, visited North Vietnam, North Korea and communist China, bearing a proposal that China and the Soviet Union should sink their differences and co-operate in pursuing the war in Vietnam to a successful conclusion. Although warmly welcomed in Hanoi and Pyongyang, the delegates met a cold rebuff from the authorities in Peking. On its return, the JCP began rapidly to sever its connections with Peking and to assert its own 'self-reliant independence' as a communist party. Its defection may indeed be traced back to the unsuccessful coup attempt in Indonesia on 30 September 1965, the failure of which suggested to the Japanese Communists that too close adherence to Chinese revolutionary strategy could have disastrous effects for a fraternal party. Miyamoto had over the previous few years been carefully fostering a mass membership, so that by 1966 his party could actually claim five times as many members as the JSP. It is understandable that he did not wish to jeopardize this newly found strength by precipitate and ill-considered action, such as might be urged upon him by his erstwhile Chinese allies.[13]

In the latter half of 1966 the JCP broke completely with the Chinese and purged those members refusing to follow the new line of independence. This involved the loss by that party of a certain amount of Chinese patronage in the form of what were known as 'friendly firm' connections. So long as the Japanese government refused to recognize communist China, the Chinese insisted that a substantial part of the considerable and increasing trade between the two countries should be channelled through what they chose to consider 'friendly' Japanese firms. This meant in practice that this trade was conducted by a quite large number of small businesses, which sought contacts with the JCP for the purpose. With the open breach, however, between the JCP and Peking, this mechanism began to break down, and some at any rate of the 'friendly firms' began to seek contacts with both pro-Chinese elements expelled from the JCP and with similarly inclined members of the JSP.[14] It is reported that a visit to China in September 1966 by a member of the Sasaki faction led to the establishment by the JSP of two trading firms, one in Tokyo and one in Ōsaka, to serve as channels for 'friendly firm' trade with Peking.[15]

In a sense the touchstone of relations between Japanese socialists and communists had been the anti-nuclear weapons movement. As we have seen, by 1964 the movement had split, with the Socialist-controlled group in total opposition to nuclear testing, while the Communist-controlled group condoned the Chinese nuclear programme (and rejection of the partial nuclear test-ban treaty) as a natural and justifiable reaction to American 'imperialist' containment of China. In 1964, however, it was already clear that the JSP left wing factions (at that time, it will be recalled, in self-proclaimed 'intra-party opposition') were not entirely satisfied with the party's stand in the anti-nuclear weapons movement.

Once he became Chairman of the JSP, Sasaki's policy towards the two wings of the anti-nuclear weapons movement was an obvious measure of his intentions. It was not long before he began to throw doubt on the party's long-standing principle that nuclear testing by any country whatever, whether capitalist or socialist, should be opposed. This, he now began to argue, unfairly discriminated against the nuclear 'have-nots' and in favour of the nuclear 'haves'.[16] As far as the anti-nuclear weapons movement was concerned, however, he acted with extreme caution, making no attempt to tamper with the platform of the wing of the movement that the Socialists controlled. By August 1966, when the JCP had already virtually severed its connections with the Chinese Communist Party, the apparent reversal in the positions of the JSP and JCP seems to have had little effect on the policies of their respective anti-nuclear movements.

The behaviour of the JSP towards both the JCP and the anti-nuclear weapons movement was intimately connected with its relations with communist China. The party had often been divided on this difficult issue. In August 1964 the left wing and right wing factions of the JSP sent 'private' delegations respectively to Peking and Moscow. To give added point to this dichotomy, the (left wing) delegation to Peking was told by its hosts that the Soviet Union ought to return to Japan the southern Kurile islands off the Hokkaidō coast, which had been taken by Soviet forces at the end of the war.[17]

In October of the same year, with full official blessing, the JSP sent a delegation to China, under the leadership of Narita. As soon as the delegates arrived in Peking they were informed, to their shock and amazement, that China had successfully conducted her first nuclear test. There was consequently a great deal of strain between them and the Chinese authorities during the course of their visit. Narita made it clear from the first that the JSP profoundly regretted the Chinese test, while understanding the provocation to which the Chinese were subjected by the American containment of China and especially by American policy in Vietnam. The solution, he suggested, was a non-nuclear zone in Asia and the Pacific, leading ultimately to universal nuclear disarmament. A Chinese spokesman, at the same meeting, proclaimed that the test was a great contribution to world peace.[18]

The final communiqué of the visit stated that the two sides agreed to differ on the question of nuclear testing, and set out their respective views. On the other hand, despite previous statements of their intention not to reaffirm in any form the 'Asanuma statement', the delegates submitted to what seems to have been intense Chinese pressure to do so. It may be assumed that they were led to believe that the Chinese would not sign any communiqué that did not reaffirm the fateful sentiment expressed by Asanuma five and a half years previously.[19]

October 1964 was in two senses a turning point in the relations of the JSP with the Soviet Union and communist China. On the one hand Soviet policy towards the party changed radically upon the retirement of Khrushchev, which occurred on the same day as the Chinese nuclear test. Previously it seems that the Soviet Union was quite active in establishing contacts with the moderates in the JSP and was successful in gaining the overall support of Eda's factional coalition. Khrushchev's successors, however, modified this policy and gave their main backing to a dissident group that had recently defected from the JCP on account of that party's failure to support the nuclear test-ban treaty. At about the same period the Chinese, who were vigorously wooing the JCP and had virtually succeeded in attaching it to their cause, apparently sought to expand their influence with the left wing of the JSP. Sasaki seems to have received some support from the Chinese from about mid-1964. From his own point of view this may well have been in part a reaction against the Soviet contacts made by the Eda faction. It was probably in this period that the Sasaki faction edged towards the pro-Chinese policies of the *Heiwa Dōshikai,* its factional ally.[20]

It was also part of a Chinese global campaign to extend their influence over communist and other left wing parties and organizations and thus to combat Soviet influence. There is evidence that on a visit to Peking in 1964 Sasaki undertook to work for the reamalgamation of the Communist- and Socialist-controlled wings of the anti-nuclear weapons movement, and thus bring to an end Socialist opposition to Chinese nuclear testing. Sasaki, however, apparently made little effort to accomplish this and the Chinese seem to have become, at least temporarily, disillusioned with him.

Sasaki was, after all, the leader of an ideologically heterogeneous faction, for which the ideological dispute between China and the Soviet Union provided serious problems. Sasaki, whatever his personal views, had to steer some kind of middle course that would not permanently antagonize a particular section of his faction. As a well-known factional manipulator, it may be assumed that he well appreciated the need for the kind of inconsistencies that this entailed. The socialist most closely identified with communist China was Okada Haruo, a member of the *Heiwa Dōshikai,* now virtually an appendage of the Sasaki faction. Okada visited Peking shortly before the January 1966 Congress, and with full Chinese endorsement seems to have played an important part in the drafting of the Action Policy. On the other hand another powerful element in the faction was the *Shakaishugi Kyōkai,* which fairly strongly supported the

Soviet side in the Sino-Soviet dispute and had been very critical of joint struggles with the JCP.[21]

There is little in all this to suggest that the Sasaki faction will necessarily continue indefinitely to maintain its present policies. They are contingent upon certain factors in the international, domestic and intra-party situation, any of which could change.

Meanwhile the Eda faction and its allies, although ousted from the leadership, sought to keep alive the neutralist tradition within the party. Thus in their criticisms of Sasaki's foreign policy, they chided him for ignoring the fact that the improvement in relations between the United States and the Soviet Union had been in large part brought about by the increased influence of 'Socialist régimes, labour movements in capitalist countries, national liberation movements, the non-aligned and neutralist policies of newly emerging nations, the international peace movement and world opinion for peace'.[22] This formulation of course bears a close resemblance to the 'third force' argument of the LSP in the early 1950s. Although as late as 1964 the Eda faction probably had the same sort of connections with the Soviet Union as the Sasaki faction had with communist China, this was now no longer the case. Indeed, international polycentric trends, both among the nations of the communist bloc and among non-aligned powers, seem to have been particularly pleasing to Eda and his associates. The party kept up contacts with a number of parties and governments, especially from these two areas, and the moderate wing of the party no doubt saw the implications of the fact that neutralism was a platform generally congenial to its foreign contacts.[23] Antipathy to a purely 'pro-Soviet' orientation has been particularly strong in the Wada and Kawakami factions.

Despite the apparent width of the policy cleavage between the Sasaki group and its opponents, the possibility of some kind of factional accommodation between them has not always been out of the question. Indeed at the January 1966 Congress it appears that only opposition from the Wada faction prevented the accomplishment of some such arrangement. At that Congress Narita (whose connections with both sides made him an ideal mediator) sought with *Sōhyō* backing to obtain general agreement for a scheme whereby Sasaki should continue as party Chairman but Narita should resign the Secretary-Generalship in favour of Sasaki's main rival Eda. Apparently he managed to persuade the main factions (including those of Sasaki and Eda) of the wisdom of this course, but Sasaki insisted that Narita should take the post of Vice-Chairman from which Wada had announced his resignation because of ill health. Since this would have meant that the Wada faction would have thereby been excluded from any share in the top executive positions, the faction announced its total rejection of Narita's proposal. This is an interesting example of how purely factional considerations have at crucial moments proved more important than matters of ideological division.

Another example of attempted factional accommodation was seen in the voting for executive positions at the January 1966 Congress. Once it was known that Sasaki and Narita had defeated Eda and his running-mate Katsumata for the top two party posts, the delegates proceeded to maintain some sort of a balance by weighting the junior executive positions against the Sasaki faction by a proportion of eleven to eight. It will be recalled that the exact reverse had occurred at the Congress of December 1964. By the Congress of December 1966, however, Sasaki had consolidated his grip on local branches of the party to the extent that not only did Sasaki increase his personal majority from nineteen to thirty-nine, but his faction won thirteen out of the nineteen junior executive positions. Since, in an endeavour to reduce the frequency of factional contests, it had now been decided to extend the tenure of junior executives from one to two years, this result further confirmed the ascendancy over the party that the Sasaki faction had managed to achieve. Once more, an attempt was made to pacify the 'outs' by creating three Vice-Chairmanships, two of which were filled with leading members of the Wada and former Kawakami factions respectively.[24] The Eda faction, however, was not represented in any senior position in the party executive, and naturally proceeded to renew the intensity of its attacks upon the Sasaki régime. Fuel was very quickly added to the flames of its opposition by the Socialist defeat in the Lower House general election of 29 January 1967, when the party's proportional and absolute share of both votes and seats fell noticeably.

Matters came to a crisis in August 1967 when Sasaki and Narita unexpectedly resigned their posts, ostensibly because of the rejection by an intransigent Central Executive Committee of their proposal to accept a mediation plan to break a Diet deadlock over the handling of a Health Insurance Bill. The delegates to a party Congress which had already been scheduled for later in the same month were thus suddenly faced with the necessity of choosing new leaders. Their choice of Chairman was Katsumata Seiichi, leader of the former Wada faction, who at the last minute had shifted his faction's allegiance from Eda to Sasaki. The new Secretary-General was Yamamoto Kōichi, Sasaki's close lieutenant and widely regarded as one of the most able—and realistic—members of his faction. Although Eda returned to office once more as Vice-Chairman, the defection from his camp of the former Wada faction was an obvious blow to his hopes of attaining the party Chairmanship in the near future. How little this particular manoeuvre had to do with issues of policy is shown by the fact that Katsumata had until recently been a persistent critic of Sasaki's pro-China policies. It seems that Sasaki's resignation may have been deliberately calculated to frustrate Eda's chances of obtaining the succession, which had begun to look brighter because of the difficulties which Sasaki's policies had caused, both for the party and for his faction.

Certainly, when considering the differences between the moderate and left wing factions, it is as well to remember also their ideological propinquity. The virulent anti-Americanism that permeated JSP pronouncements under Sasaki's leadership was in tune with the dominant tradition of the party's rhetoric. In many ways the similarities between the Sasaki faction and its 'moderate' opponents outweigh the differences. As we have seen, the party's neutralist policies have repeatedly slipped over into a one-sided attack on the American military presence in the Far East. Both sides of the party have usually agreed that American military and economic strategy in Asia both endangers and exploits Japan, and also encourages the Japanese government in its allegedly militarist course. All JSP factions have regarded abolition of the Mutual Security Treaty as the most urgent and vital aim the party could possibly have in present circumstances. But they have also all without exception consistently attacked the United States for her occupation of Okinawa (especially its use as a military base), her support for the Nationalist government on Taiwan (which all agree should revert to mainland control), her policies in Korea and Vietnam and pressure on Japan not to trade with Peking. The party has been completely united on issues such as opposition to the treaty between Japan and South Korea, and to American nuclear-powered submarines calling at Japanese ports.

Both sides, moreover, inherit the same type of Marxist ideology, although the younger generation of party activists is rather less interested in ideology than were its elders, and more concerned with practical politics. It would be strange, however, if Sasaki and his closest colleagues, being mostly of the 'pre-war' generation of socialists, had ceased to be imbued with the thinking of the *Rōnō-ha* school in which they were reared. For reasons discussed earlier, the *Rōnō-ha* strategies of revolution are quite different from the Maoist strategies, which at certain periods have commended themselves to the JCP.

It has already been argued that the most important reason why the Sasaki faction led the JSP in its recent direction relates to American involvement in Vietnam. It is, however, quite possible that other factors are also present. Was the faction seeking Chinese funds for electoral and other purposes? Rumours to this effect were circulating in June-July 1967. It is possible that the above-mentioned establishment by the JSP of trading firms as channels for 'friendly firm' trade with Peking may have had some such ancillary purpose. In the latter half of 1966 the JSP faced uncomfortable charges that its leaders were themselves not immune to the kind of corruption of which the LDP stood accused. Donations to the party from business circles, which had provided it with a substantial income over many years, were therefore, for reasons of the party's conscience and reputation, now perhaps in jeopardy and an alternative source of funds was needed.

However this may be, the pro-China policies of the Sasaki faction do seem to have made some sense considered as political strategy and given the faction's pervading suspicion of the United States. The ideal of a China friendly to Japan is one that has in the past always appealed strongly to Japanese intellectuals, whereas the Soviet Union has never had the same mystique, being often the object of fear and dislike. A common culture, vast trade possibilities, the moral duty of repaying the debt incurred for past military aggression—these were the main ingredients in a commonly encountered Japanese view of China. It was frequently assumed that communism in China was only skin deep and that it was in practice modified by the traditional nature of Chinese civilization.[25] It followed from these attitudes that China could not be a threat, that her nuclear weapons were purely defensive and that the Americans were chiefly at fault for her aggressive posture.

It seems significant that Sasaki should have stepped up his overt support for China after the JCP had defected from the Chinese camp. This defection meant that otherwise no significant section of the left wing in Japan would have been aligned with China, whereas the cause of closer Japan-China relations had many supporters, not least in the business world and the more left wing factions of the ruling LDP. Sasaki's policies may, therefore, have had the added purpose of filling the vacuum caused by the defection of the JCP, in the belief that in so doing his faction would gain the support and good will of a substantial body of opinion. One persistent theme in his speeches was the need to prepare the party for participation in a coalition government which he expected to be formed in the early 1970s.[26] It seems that, in his calculations, a foreign policy based on the aim of improving relations with China would stand a greater chance than any other of containing the inevitably centrifugal tendencies of such a coalition, especially if the 'pro-China' factions of the LDP were to break away from their present party and take part.

The fact, however, that Sasaki's policies appeared to be so extreme tended to alienate rather than attract other parties. After the January 1967 general election the DSP strongly dissociated itself from the JSP and called it a 'second Communist Party'. Moreover—and this is perhaps the key point—the Chinese Cultural Revolution has undoubtedly alienated a great deal of formerly sympathetic Japanese opinion (whether temporarily or permanently remains to be seen), and its more hysterical features appear to have surprised and disturbed Sasaki himself, who seems to have been recently trying to extricate himself from his 'Chinese' predicament.

The new Katsumata-Yamamoto leadership is clearly pursuing a rather more moderate line, and must tentatively be regarded as more 'realistic' than its predecessor.

Neutralism, as a pillar of JSP foreign policy, has not been abandoned. An outline of the party's long-term goals in foreign policy, put out with official sanction in mid-1966, reiterated all the old neutralist aims.[27] Moreover, the factions opposing Sasaki still cling to a neutralist position much like that presented by Eda in the early 1960s. The frustrations of recent policy, together with the vagaries of factional conflict, mean that it could once more very quickly become the main stream of the party's foreign policy. On the other hand, Chinese pressures, the failures of neutralism elsewhere in Asia, and above all the Vietnam war, have created within the party a militancy basically unfavourable to neutralist policies.

11

ASPECTS OF THE NEUTRALIST
BLUEPRINT

For the Japanese Socialists neutralism has been many things:
a policy, a slogan, a factional bone of contention, a means of
embarrassing the government; party leaders have championed
it, paid lip service to it and obliquely criticized it. Attitudes to
current concrete issues, such as the Sino-Soviet dispute, have
fluctuated with changes in the leadership. Yet the actual content
of the party's official neutralist policy has changed remarkably
little. The Ishibashi plan of 1966[1] is the same in essentials as the
1959 blueprint for 'positive neutrality', which in turn differed
little from the neutralist schemes of the Left Socialists in the
first half of the 1950s. This is partly because all the fundamental
proposals involved remain completely unrealized. Japan is still
a party to the Treaty of Mutual Co-operation and Security
between the United States of America and Japan (19 January
1960). Her 'Self-Defence' Forces have been built up despite the
Constitution, Okinawa is still an American base, communist
China remains unrecognized by the Japanese government and
is outside the UN, there is still no peace treaty with the Soviet
Union, Korea remains divided and Nationalist China a separate
state.

Thus the Asian *détente* which was to accompany the neutralization of Japan has failed to come about. The United States is
still in the area in strength, and until her troops show some
signs of departing the goal of neutralism can make little headway. In these circumstances much Japanese socialist argumenta-
tion has a rather abstract, theoretical quality, untempered by
concrete experiences.

Nevertheless, certain aspects of the socialist vision as the party expresses it are worth investigating in detail, since they reveal a certain attitude to world affairs and to Japan's international position. The two issues which most obviously claim our attention are these: Once Japan were to declare herself neutralist, how would her own security be guaranteed? And what kind of contribution could a neutralist Japan make to world peace and security, especially in Asia? Briefly, the socialist answer to the first of these questions is that Japan, by the abolition of the Mutual Security Treaty, would become more, not less, secure, while to the second they would answer that by changing the direction of her foreign policy in so radical a fashion she could have a very salutary influence indeed on Asian and world developments.

In considering the first question, it must be recalled that the Socialists (as outlined in chapter 1) have rejected the Security Treaty as intolerable on at least four counts. It is an unconvincing guarantee of security (the Americans cannot be trusted to defend Japan), prejudicial to Japanese interests and independence, dangerously provocative to China and the Soviet Union, and from the point of view of national security essentially unnecessary.

Their hitherto consistent advocacy of total, or near total, Japanese disarmament is naturally bound up with the last two of these arguments. The removal of the Mutual Security Treaty would reduce tensions so that there would be no threat from the mainland. Since danger could hardly come from any other direction (except in case of total nuclear war, against which Japan could not possibly hope to have effective defence) there was no point in having armed forces. In any case, armed forces were positively undesirable, since they kept alive profoundly reactionary tendencies and—given the history of Japanese militarism—could well develop into a threat to the civilian government, especially if the latter were socialist.

For these reasons the problem of making arrangements for Japan's defence has been treated somewhat lightly by the JSP. That is not to say, however, that they have not considered it at all. A number of solutions have at various times been suggested, of which the idea of a four-power treaty to guarantee Japanese neutrality has been official party policy since 1955. In order to

understand more fully the presuppositions upon which this and
other schemes have been based, let us examine some of them
in detail.

One point of view heard occasionally in the early 1950s was
that an unarmed Japan could be defended by passive resistance.
This particularly appealed to socialists on the extreme left (such
as Professor Sakisaka) who believed most intensely in the power
of organized labour. Taking his examples, as was his wont, from
German political experience between the wars, Sakisaka argued
that the resistance put up by German labour both to the French
invasion of the Ruhr and to the counter-revolutionary Kapp
putsch, were adequate demonstrations of what could be done
by a determined and well-led trade union movement.[2] It is particularly significant that this argument was directed against a
group within the *Shakaishugi Kyōkai* that favoured the establishment of a revolutionary 'people's militia'. Sakisaka doubted
that the Japanese working class could maintain or even keep
control of an effective armed force, which would be only too
likely to become an instrument of capitalist oppression. He no
doubt had in mind the miserable and amateurish failure of the
JCP in its current alleged attempts to stage armed uprisings
against the American forces. At any rate he maintained that a
large scale pacifist movement (by implication a movement
against constitutional revision) was a golden opportunity for the
establishment of socialism.

Not all who wrote in this vein were inclined to take the argument to such a relentlessly Marxist conclusion as Sakisaka. With
others, the pacifist, rather than the Marxist, sentiment prevailed.[3] At this period a straightforward determination to avoid
rearmament was to be found among many socialists who would
not have called themselves Marxists, and even among some
who would.

Passive resistance was seldom advocated after the Occupation
had ended, and never figured in official Socialist policy. A more
persistent argument, however, was that an effort of national will
would be required to defend neutralism, such as the Swiss had
exhibited over centuries of experience with neutrality, but
Belgium had allegedly failed to show in 1914.[4] What this was
to mean in the absence of armed forces remained obscure, but

the logic of the situation naturally suggested some form of external protection or guarantee. In the immediate post-war period some writers, contemplating the disarmament of Japan, thought she would need to rely on UN 'collective security'.[5] Apart from the prohibition on military forces contained in article 9 of the 1946 Constitution, the preamble of the same document contained a passage which could be interpreted to mean that Japan should entrust her security to the UN.[6] This argument, however, did not long survive the advent of the cold war and the consequent demise of early hopes for the establishment of a really powerful UN force backed by all the major powers. Later JSP policy statements spoke in Utopian terms of a world controlled by the UN[7] but there is little suggestion that this was meant to be taken seriously as a practical proposition.

One proposal was, however, put forward in 1959 by Sakamoto Yoshikazu, a university professor sympathetic to the JSP, who sought to involve the UN directly in the defence of a neutralist Japan. His proposal was that a UN force, paid for entirely by the Japanese government, should be stationed permanently in Japan. Moreover the Japanese Self-Defence Forces should be reduced in size and merged with the UN force under UN command.[8] It is evident that the scheme was carefully designed to meet anticipated objections from the JSP stemming from the party's fundamental attitudes to foreign policy.

Thus Sakamoto was at pains to point out that his proposal did not envisage the stationing on Japanese soil of forces from any of the major powers, but that the operation should be conducted rather like that staged in Egypt after the Suez crisis, and not like the American-dominated expedition to Korea. He thus recognized the increased power of neutralist nations within the United Nations Organization, a point which might have been expected to appeal to a neutralist party. The force would not, he stressed, be equipped under any circumstances with nuclear weapons.

A further aspect of Sakamoto's proposal will be discussed, but at this point it is sufficient to note that although it excited some favourable comment from the public,[9] it hardly attracted any support within the JSP. This suggests, among other things, that the party was not primarily concerned either with the UN or with the hypothetical problem of guaranteeing Japan's neutralism. Policies that would serve to make neutralism possible were of far more immediate concern to them.

In any case, the party had already proposed a four-power treaty of non-aggression between Japan, the United States, the Soviet Union and China. It was hoped to approach this by stages: the Security Treaty should be abolished, bilateral non-aggression treaties should be concluded with the Soviet Union, China and the United States, and finally a four-power treaty could be expected to materialize. (Sakamoto, incidentally, showed considerable scepticism about the whole idea.) As early as 1950 the desirability of obtaining some sort of international guarantee from nations on both sides of the cold war was tentatively discussed,[10] but the 'Locarno' idea did not take final shape until Socialist reunification in 1955.

In order to show that such a scheme was practicable, two things had to be demonstrated with some plausibility. First, that members of the conflicting power blocs would have an interest in combining to guarantee the security of an unarmed neutralist Japan. Second, that such a guarantee, if implemented, had a reasonable chance of proving effective and permanent.

Neutralists, therefore, sought to show that it was in the interests of the major powers to have Japan both neutral and disarmed, and that capitalist and communist nations might be willing to merge their differences and agree in guaranteeing Japan's security for the sake of preventing her resurgence as a militarist power. This was sometimes based on the attitudes of the Allied powers concerning Japan, as expressed in the Potsdam Declaration. Their determination, shown in that document, to keep Japan disarmed, was seen as evidence that they might be prepared to enter into some kind of collective guarantee of her security.[11]

In 1950 China and the Soviet Union signed the Treaty of Friendship, which contained a clause specifying mutual defence against Japanese aggression. It thus became one of the goals of JSP neutralism to persuade the two signatories to rescind at least this clause of their treaty. After Japan regained independence Japanese socialists often argued that this might be accomplished, and that both China and the Soviet Union might be prepared to guarantee Japan's security, as the price of ending the Security Treaty and effecting the withdrawal of American bases.[12] The Sino-Soviet dispute of the 1960s did not substantially alter official JSP policy in this regard, although it was recognized that the 1950 Treaty of Friendship had become a dead letter.

Whether a collective guarantee of Japan's security would be likely to prove effective if it could be obtained was a question on which the JSP was characteristically vague. Now one specialist in international law (quite unconnected with the party) spelled out very carefully the nature of such a guarantee in the case of Switzerland. To have a collective guarantee was, he maintained, absolutely essential and indeed the principal characteristic of 'permanent neutrality'. This did not accord with the comparative lack of emphasis placed upon the question by the JSP. While the concept of a four-power treaty of guarantee played its part in facilitating the achievement of Socialist unification in 1955, and although it has always figured in the party's foreign policy statements since, it was removed from the realm of immediate aims by a process of reasoning which went some way towards recognizing the difficulties likely to be involved in its realization. This reasoning sharply distinguished neutralism from Swiss-type 'permanent neutrality'. Thus one party spokesman distinguished 'neutralization formalized by treaty' from 'positive neutrality'. A four-power treaty (like UN collective security), was, he argued, a rather distant ideal, and thus the Liberal-Democrats, who dismissed it as impracticable dreaming, missed the point.

> The foreign policy which is urgently required for Japan at present is a positive neutralist policy to accomplish what is possible in the situation in which Japan is placed . . . and gradually to widen its scope . . . This is the correct way of achieving neutralism, since neutralism is not something that will be brought about suddenly by treaty or declaration.[13]

Thus neutralism was considered a policy sufficient unto itself scarcely requiring to be hedged round with guarantees. Nevertheless, socialists frequently expressed optimism about the possibility of achieving a four-power treaty once the JSP actually got into power.[14]

The second major question to which we must now turn relates to Japanese Socialist ideas about the contribution that a neutralist Japan could make to Asian—and ultimately to world—peace and security. The JSP programme met persistent criticism for its alleged irresponsibility and self-centredness, and the party was consequently at pains to emphasize the 'positive' nature of its thinking. It is interesting to trace the stages through which this controversy has gone.

In 1949 and 1950 the argument centred on the assertion of Yokota Kisaburō (a non-socialist academic lawyer) that in an age of international co-operation and collective sanctions by the UN neutrality was out of date, and should be equated with egoistic nationalism.[15] The fact that Switzerland had not joined the UN was adduced by Yokota to show that Japan too should not be able to combine neutrality with membership of the world body.

Neutralists either accepted this challenge on its own terms and sought to show that their policies were perfectly compatible with duties towards the UN, or in some cases they argued that Japan should not seek UN membership. This latter argument rested on the assumption that as a UN member Japan would be unlikely to obtain permission to opt out of collective sanctions, while sanctions, at any rate if they involved armed force, were incompatible with both disarmament and neutral status.[16] Ryū Shintarō, editor of the *Asahi*, maintained that even in the unlikely event of Japan being admitted to UN membership (actually she was not admitted until 1957) Japan would be in a quandary over sanctions. Without armed forces of her own to contribute to military sanctions, her co-operation would have to take an economic form, or consist in the presentation of military bases. This would mean that Japan would be effectively aligned with one side in the cold war and would have to fight against the other despite her total absence of armed forces.[17]

Despite this kind of argument neutralists increasingly held that membership of the UN was not incompatible with a neutralist Japan. The influential intellectual study group *Heiwa*

Mondai Danwakai was already arguing in late 1950 that while in deference to the interests of the major powers the Security Council veto should not be tampered with, the say of the smaller, non-committed nations should be increased.[18] It was clear by this time that the UN was not capable of fulfilling the role originally envisaged for it, and that therefore there was no *de facto* bar to the entry of a nation professing neutralism.[19] Neutralists remained, however, very insistent that Japan should join the UN only on the understanding that her constitutional position absolved her from the duty of participating in UN peace-keeping operations, or of granting portions of her territory for the purpose of military bases.[20]

So far as UN peace-keeping is concerned this has represented a position common to both Socialists and Liberal-Democrats. Successive Japanese governments have held that the Constitution precludes Japanese participation in UN peace-keeping expeditions, although there have been recent suggestions that this policy might be marginally revised.[21]

There are indications that some socialists have experienced disquiet at the apparently negative implications of this ban. Sakamoto's above-mentioned plan for a permanent UN force to be stationed in Japan was devised in part to solve this problem. With the existing Self-Defence Forces cut back and put under UN command, the constitutional objections to Japanese participation in UN peace-keeping would, he argued, no longer apply. Also, his proposal that the UN force should be entirely financed by Japan, was virtually the only intimation by a left wing politician or academic that Japan should substantially pay for her own defence.

As the Self-Defence Forces have been gradually built up into a modern and sophisticated military establishment, the JSP has come to recognize that its policy of abolishing them or substantially cutting them back might run up against considerable difficulties. The party, as we have seen, has been traditionally suspicious of military power and uncertain that the principle of civilian control was being, or could expect to be, successfully applied. In recent policy statements, therefore, the party has spoken of the need to move cautiously in this policy once the JSP came to power. Military reductions would have to be carried out gradually, with due regard to the relative balance of power and popular support between the civilian government and the military command, and also to the international situation.[22]

The conversion of the Self-Defence Forces into 'forces for peaceful construction' has been official Socialist policy since 1955. In a recent move, however, it has been proposed that such forces could be used to help in the development of South-east Asia. This is significant in the sense that it entails, though in a minimal and theoretical sense, a departure from the party's extreme reluctance to contemplate the despatch of forces abroad. There seems little doubt that the situation in Vietnam has given rise to this proposal.

Another persistent idea has been that of a non-nuclear zone in Asia and the western Pacific, introduced in 1959. In its origin it clearly reflected concern with the possibility that nuclear weapons might be introduced into Japan, but the 'positive' side, that is the desire to promote nuclear disarmament by stages, is also often stated. The neutralization and reunification of both Korea and Vietnam has now been tied in with this idea. It is envisaged that a solution to the divisions of these two countries will enable them to be included in a non-nuclear zone including Japan, India, Pakistan, the Philippines and all the countries of South-east Asia.[23]

The reader may wonder whether these proposals are meant to be taken literally, as signposts to what the party expects to be able to accomplish if it is elected to power. Or do they, as the party's critics sometimes suggest, serve to mask an ulterior and very different purpose in the language of Utopia? In the present writer's opinion several ends are accomplished by these programmes. First, their declamatory nature is designed to satisfy many party members whose outlook is governed more by idealistic and pacifist principles than by either Marxism or political ambition. This no doubt also applies to some in the electorate. Second, they tend to represent a common denominator of agreement between the factions. The function of the four-power treaty concept in bringing Right and Left Socialists together in 1955 has already been discussed. Generally speaking, it is easier for the factions to agree on remote aims than on immediate aims. Third, however (and given the above limitations) they are part of an attempt, particularly by members of the party's Foreign Policy Bureau, to outline a genuine neutralist alternative to the government's foreign policy. The atmosphere of 'cloud-cuckoo-land' which sometimes pervades JSP statements of ultimate intention should not be allowed to obscure from view the relatively hard-headed pragmatism of many party officials and Diet members. Given the limitations imposed upon them by factional conflict and ideological considerations, it is remarkable how down-to-earth is their reasoning and how broad the extent of their information on foreign affairs. One should not, of course, take this too far: the fact that for a long period the party's Foreign Policy Bureau was dominated by the particularly pragmatic Wada faction obscured the relative lack of power possessed by that faction at the party centre.

One aspect of neutralist thinking in the JSP concerned the international position which neutralists hoped Japan would be able to assume. One of their persistent and most effective criticisms of successive Japanese governments was their failure to make Japan's voice felt in a positive way in world councils, particularly but by no means only at the UN. The party maintained that this inactivity was a result of Japan's political and economic dependence on the United States. If Japan became neutralist, therefore, what kind of political role would she be able to play in international affairs? If we leave aside the party's visionary statements and examine more mundane evidence, an interesting pattern emerges.

The 'third force' neutralism adopted by Left Socialists in the early 1950s, mainly inspired by India, was premised on the assumption that Japan was a power of the third rank, and that if she became neutralist she would in no sense be a dominant force among the 'developing' nations that had already embraced neutralism. It was no doubt thought necessary to give an assurance of this kind to countries of South-east Asia, where Japan was still regarded with strong suspicion for her actions during the war.[24] It should also be remembered that she was not admitted to the UN until 1957.

More recent Socialist formulations of neutralism, however, have laid more stress on Japan's economic strength and potential leadership capacity, implying that she should be able to exercise leadership over other, weaker, neutralist countries. Although the precise form which such leadership would take was never explicitly stated (and in particular the military aspect remained obscure), a noticeable shift of emphasis occurred. This had certain ideological overtones and did not represent a conscious change of viewpoint. At least three elements were involved: disillusion with the failure of socialist parties in most Asian countries, an increasing tendency to take ideological lessons from the European Left, and an awareness of the political implications of Japan's economic growth.

Disillusion with Asian socialism expressed itself particularly in regret at the failure of the ASC after the high hopes invested in it by both Japanese socialist parties in 1953. The fact that the decline of specifically socialist political parties in Asia (Singapore constituting an exception) could be plausibly blamed on 'imperialism' and 'neo-colonialism', did not diminish the sense of the disappointment of high hopes.

The second element was a tendency to take lessons from the European Left, once the enthusiasm for Asian socialism had subsided. One example is the influence of the Italian Communist Party upon Structural Reform. In foreign policy the Yugoslav brand of neutralism was treated with a good deal of interest, and the De Gaulle phenomenon was not without influence in the party, as indeed in Japan as a whole.

The third element was the newly awakened consciousness of national strength by the 1960s. Japan's position as a major industrial and trading nation, treated with respect by advanced countries and envy by developing ones, had been established by a combination of rapid economic growth, assiduous diplomacy and restraint in trading practices. Japanese economic assistance in the development of South-east Asia, and her active participation in regional development organizations such as the Asian Development Bank was now widely discussed and to a limited extent acted upon. Some of the confidence and national self-respect which this engendered affected the JSP, whose neutralist wing, at least, came to see Japan as a leader of Asian neutralism and a powerful leader of the neutralist countries in the UN. Of course most socialists were reticent about the possibility of a clash of interests between communist China and a neutralist Japan, as this involved major unresolved problems concerning the current leadership of the JSP. It is, however, not fanciful to see the 1966 proposal to send elements of the Self-Defence Forces—suitably disarmed and demilitarized—to South-east Asia on missions of economic construction, as a reflection of concern with Japan's leadership role. Socialists frequently spoke of the elimination of American influence from Asia in terms of the national advantages this would bring to Japan—national advantages, that is, which included Japanese prestige and influence in the area.

The obverse of this factor was that some Socialists interviewed in 1962–3 took a rather disparaging view of the failure of Indian neutralism to maintain itself intact in the face of difficulties with her neighbours. Their attribution of this failure to India's economic weakness implied that Japan, in contrast, would be in a much stronger position to pursue an effectively neutralist policy. One leading official of the JSP Foreign Policy Bureau, and a particular enthusiast for Yugoslavia, favourably contrasted the 'positive' neutralist policies of Tito which had enabled Yugoslavia to play a significant and worthwhile role in world affairs, with the 'passive' neutralism of India which had registered a succession of failures.[25] One may well discern behind this thinking the image of Yugoslavia as the sole European neutralist (Sweden, Switzerland and Austria were 'old-fashioned' neutrals, and thus did not count) contrasted, despite her relative economic backwardness in the European context, with India, poverty-stricken, conservative and Asiatic.

In conclusion it may be noted that these views (or the attitudes that underlay them) have much in common with opinions generally accepted in Japan, about the course Japanese foreign policy should take. Socialists are, so to speak, in the main stream of the contemporary Japanese foreign policy consciousness, despite obvious peculiarities of their own. The government in principle accepts (although it does not always act on) American urgings that Japan should shoulder some portion of the American burden of responsibilities in Asia, while interpreting this essentially in economic terms and rejecting any suggestion of a Japanese military commitment in Vietnam or elsewhere.

This indicates that Socialists and Liberal-Democrats are not so far apart in foreign policy as was sometimes supposed. Moreover, despite differing attitudes concerning the causes of the Vietnam war, both earnestly desire Japanese mediation to end it.[26] Neither is prepared to forego the expanding trade with communist China, which in 1966 reached approximately $US600m both ways, or 4 per cent of Japan's total trade. The Liberal-Democrats, on the other hand, are themselves divided on the question of *political* relations with Peking, the related problem of Taiwan and the extent to which communist China represents a military threat to Japan.

A more 'positive' Japanese foreign policy in Asia, whether inspired by left wing or right wing parties, is unlikely to be realized while the American military commitment in Asia remains at a high level because of Vietnam. Events in that country have slowed down the tendency for Japan to increase her independence of the United States. Little progress, for instance, has been recorded in the reversion to Japan of administrative rights over Okinawa, although hopes for this were considerable during the Kennedy era. It was American military procurements for Vietnam that helped to pull the Japanese economy out of its recession of 1964–5. Moreover, as we have seen, the whole Vietnam situation, especially as it affected Japan's freedom of action, has caused frustrations and an extremist reaction in the JSP. It is reasonable to suppose, however, that if a settlement or even a de-escalation of the Vietnam conflict is achieved in the foreseeable future, the trend towards Japanese independence of the United States may resume. Whether Japan is likely to achieve and comfortably maintain an independent position as a major political power, concomitant with the economic status she has already achieved, is not easy to say. In the opinion of one writer Japan has been more successful as a dependent or middle power than as a great power; a substantial American withdrawal from Asia may jeopardize Japan's position unless she increases her military strength and improves relations with China and the Soviet Union.[27] However this may be, it does seem that both main parties are at one in wanting a more independent and powerful role for Japan in the councils of Asia and the world.

There remains the question of possible future socialist attitudes to armament and defence. It is still very difficult to determine whether the JSP will continue to think worthwhile its fundamentalist anti-armaments posture, which was born in the intensely pacifist atmosphere that followed the nuclear bombing of Hiroshima and Nagasaki and the fire raids on Tokyo. It seems quite possible that the party might modify its attitudes on conventional arms, but a change on the question of nuclear weapons would require something approaching a revolution in the party's traditional foreign policy. For the time being this must be seen as highly unlikely. Perfectly genuine anti-nuclear sentiment remains strong within the party's ranks, and will probably continue to do so.

12

THE JSP: A SOCIALIST PARTY WITH
A DIFFERENCE

The JSP is a political party professing socialism. As such it merits comparison with socialist and labour parties elsewhere. Seen in this context the foreign policy of the JSP is quite unusual, as the Socialist International has pointed out on occasions. In contrast, nearly all the socialist parties of Western Europe, although prepared to explore further than most of their conservative opponents schemes for limited neutrality, 'disengagement', or more recently an 'opening to the East', have for the most part supported the aims of NATO.[1] (The socialists, of course, have now been outdone by the Gaullists.)

An exception to the general rule is (or was) the Italian Socialist Party (PSI) of Nenni. No other European socialist party since World War II has been so friendly to the communists, nor so hostile to the western alliance. Here perhaps is a party that can be set alongside the JSP. The two parties have been similar in their general orientation, in the issues dividing them internally and in aspects of their factional structures. Naturally enough there are also significant points of difference, but the extent of their similarity suggests the presence of underlying common factors.

Three aspects of their development were of crucial importance and are particularly worth comparing. One is the broad political context in which they respectively operated. Here the similarities between them are remarkable. Another is the nature of the issues which they respectively faced, and the responses which they gave. Here again there are strong similarities, especially in the way the same issues divided both parties into comparable factional groupings. Finally, we shall discuss the character of factionalism in the two parties, where the differences will be found to be at least as intriguing as the similarities.

Our first sphere of comparison is the broad political context in which each party functioned.

In both Italy and Japan competitive party politics were resumed at the end of World War II after periods of near-totalitarian government which denied a legal existence to socialist parties. In Italy, organized socialism was suppressed in 1926 soon after Mussolini established one-party rule, and most of its leaders spent their next twenty years in exile or inactivity. In Japan the period of single-party dictatorship was much shorter (1940–5), but in the twenty years before 1940 socialism had an extremely difficult time, subject as it was to crippling legal restrictions and coming under increasing nationalist influence and control.

Certainly before 1923 the history of socialism in the two countries was strikingly different. Whereas in Japan the socialist movement of the first two decades of the twentieth century was confined to small numbers of individuals, mostly intellectuals, socialism in Italy was a strong and deeply rooted mass movement. For instance in the revolutionary atmosphere of 1919 the PSI emerged from a general election as the largest parliamentary party, securing 156 seats as against 352 seats shared between nine other groups. At this time in Japan, despite disturbed conditions and spontaneous outbursts of working class dissatisfaction, no socialist party was in existence.

Nevertheless the fact that each movement had been suppressed and persecuted over a long period effectively meant that for many years neither had had any large-scale organizational experience, nor had either participated in government. This tended to perpetuate ideological quarrels between the leaders, who worked in a kind of vacuum. Another effect was to enhance the prestige of the revolutionary and dynamic left against the reformist and democratic right.

A further point at which similarities may be observed is in the colour of the respective governments of the two countries after World War II. The virtual monopoly of power by conservative administrations in Japan was matched in Italy by a succession of right-of-centre coalitions. The experience of both Italy and Japan here contrasts with that of other European countries: Great Britain, which enjoyed a Labour government between 1945 and 1951 and again from 1964; France, whose Socialist Party participated in a number of cabinets of the Fourth Republic; and Scandinavia, where administrations of the left predominated. (West Germany, however, was in this respect similar to Japan and Italy.)

Similarities between the two countries also existed in economic development. Both, after the period of recovery from the war, endured lower living standards than prevailed in northern and western Europe. In both, an advanced industrial economy had come comparatively late, but the post-war period saw rapid economic growth and diversification. In both, again, average per capita income, and especially incomes of industrial workers, was rising fast.

In sum, therefore, before World War II both the PSI and the JSP were unable to make headway against persecution by dictatorial and anti-democratic governments. After the war ended they were both condemned to a limbo of perpetual opposition, facing conservative governments that they considered reactionary. Both parties had behind them a proletariat at a relatively early and turbulent stage of its development, which was, however, rapidly coming to assimilate the wealth and attitudes of a mature industrial society. It is hardly surprising if these factors tended to produce a more radical socialist movement than grew up in other countries whose socialist parties had long enjoyed full legal status, had post-war experience of ruling their respective peoples, and where for some years the fruits of advanced industrialization had been widely shared.

The second area of comparison relates to certain post-war issues and the response which each party made. Both were divided among themselves about the international alignment of their respective countries, and about their own relations with international socialist movements. In both cases this was related not only to foreign policy as such, but also to fundamental ideological divisions deriving from the early days of their respective movements. On the extreme right of both Japanese and Italian socialist movements there was a faction which advocated reformist 'Fabian' socialism, was intransigently opposed to communism and was prepared, in certain circumstances, to enter into coalition governments with conservative parties. The position of the Nishio faction of the JSP which took the party into the coalition of 1947-8 (the failure of which led to the ascendancy of the left wing in the party) has already been described. In 1947 the Saragat faction broke away from the main stream of the Italian socialist movement and formed a separate party, based on very similar principles, which subsequently participated in conservative-dominated administrations from 1948-51. On the extreme left of both parties there were factions advocating a close alliance with the communists. Because of the greater strength of the Communist Party (PCI) in Italy,[2] the view that proletarian unity should prevail over differences with the communists was stronger among Italian than Japanese socialists; the PSI formed a united front with the PCI in order to fight the 1948 general election, and retained close ties with it until about 1956. After 1953 when the PSI was already moving away from the communist alliance, the extreme left position in the party was occupied by a group of 'Fusionists',[3] whose views were very similar to those of the extreme left factions of the JSP.

The extent of ideological division within both parties was shown in their relations with the Socialist International. In March 1949 COMISCO (the predecessor of the Socialist International) expelled the PSI for its pact with the communists. Significantly enough, however, the PSI itself was already divided over the issue of relations with this body into three main factions. On the right a faction advocating reunion with the Saragat Socialists and a final break with the communists supported close relations with it in much the same terms[4] as were used by the RSP in Japan during the early 1950s. The faction spoke in terms which implied a 'third force' of socialist parties (or preferably socialist states), while rejecting the idea of a neutralist Italy outside the western military alliance.

On the left of the PSI the faction which had led the party into its electoral alliance with the communists totally rejected COMISCO and directed its sympathies towards the Soviet bloc.

In between left and right a centre faction adopted a position not unlike the neutralism of the LSP in Japan during the early 1950s. True to this outlook, it maintained that the party should

remain a member of COMISCO, but act within it as a minority critical of its pro-western, anti-Soviet policies.[5]
This closely corresponded to views frequently expressed by the left wing factions of the JSP in relation to the Socialist International. At periods when these factions were dominant (especially in the LSP 1951-5, and the JSP after the secession of the DSP in 1959) the party was outspokenly critical of the Socialist International, while not actually renouncing its membership. The grounds for JSP criticism, as for that of the PSI, were largely ideological: the International, by advocating reformism in domestic politics and anti-communism in foreign policy, misunderstood the local situation, which required a more intransigent and committed struggle against domination by foreign and domestic 'monopoly capital'.

The resilience of Marxist tradition in the two parties was shown in the predominance of a left wing which firmly rejected gradualism or 'reformism', shunned any compromise or coalition with 'bourgeois' parties (depending instead upon the might of the proletariat to produce revolution) and was strongly influenced by pacifism. In foreign policy, therefore, they tended to be sympathetic with the communist bloc and to ignore or play down the totalitarian element in communist régimes, despite their own official attachment to 'democracy'. Moreover their ideological anti-Americanism led them to reject military agreements with the United States, and to advocate either neutralism or a close association with the communist countries. A fundamental similarity in the foreign policy issues facing the two parties was thus matched by a parallel ideological approach.

The third sphere of comparison is the character of factionalism within the two parties. Both parties were composed of a number of discrete factions, each possessing a distinct organization of its own and competing strongly with rival factions. In the PSI, as in the JSP, a number of 'left' factions of divergent origin combined against an equally diverse group of 'right' factions, so that factional struggles were conducted at the level both of the individual faction and of the factional coalition.

Nevertheless, deeper analysis shows that these similarities mask important differences. This can be seen especially if we compare the factional balance in the two parties over the post-war period. The JSP moved from right wing dominance after the war, through a time of increasing left wing dominance (1949–60), into a period of factional recasting, which resulted in a 'neo-right wing' ascendant at first but eventually challenged successfully by the 'old-fashioned' left (1960–6).

The PSI, on the other hand, after the Saragat secession of 1947, entered a phase of extreme leftist dominance, during which the party was closely allied with the PCI (1949–56). From 1953, however, the Autonomist factions, which wanted to sever ties with the communists, were gaining strength at the expense of those who wished to continue in close association with them.[6] The Hungarian revolt in 1956 gave added impetus to the Autonomist ascendancy, whose leadership worked patiently for the formation of a coalition government of the Christian Democrats, the Saragat Socialists and the PSI. This aim, after many setbacks, was finally accomplished in 1963.

It is difficult to overestimate the distance which the PSI had travelled from its close alliance with the communists in the early 1950s to its co-operation with the Christian Democrats in the early 1960s. In comparison the path trodden by the JSP seems one of intense conservatism, of failure to adapt to socio-economic changes and of inability to take itself seriously as a viable alternative government.

It is surprising at first sight that these two parties, initially so remarkably similar, should have developed in such different directions. This, in our view, is to be explained less in terms of underlying ideological or political divergence, than of basic differences in political behaviour as between Japan and Italy. These concern the character of factions and their leadership, and ultimately the relationship between parties, factions, candidates and voters.

It must be admitted that the political conditions facing the JSP and the PSI differed in one important respect, namely the existence of a far stronger Communist Party in Italy than in Japan, a Communist Party, moreover, which dominated the main trade union federation. It is true that the PSI leaders led their party into alliance with the PCI at least partly because, as the weaker of two 'mass parties' they did not wish to lose support from the charge of splitting the proletarian front. The

JCP, on the other hand, for the most part received such a small vote that pressure from the extreme left wing of the much more powerful JSP for closer relations with the communists could be safely ignored by the rest of the party.

The fact, however, that the PSI was initially tied to the PCI and yet broke away from it in such a decisive fashion, does not diminish the strength of leadership which was necessary to guide the party along such a path.

A comparison of the leadership of the PSI with that of the JSP indicates one important element lacking in the latter which was present in the former. The PSI possessed a truly charismatic leader in the person of Nenni. The ability of a leader of this type to prevail over entrenched party bureaucrats by his appeal to the mass of party adherents, is a well-documented phenomenon.[7] The career of Nenni is an excellent illustration. Although he was leader of the left faction just after the war, and was one of the most important initiators of the pact with the communists, he later lent the weight of his authority to the Autonomist cause and successfully (though not without a hard struggle) confronted the powerful bureaucratic apparatus which during the heyday of left wing ascendancy had imitated the communists to the extent of stifling free intra-party discussion and debate.

The JSP did not at any stage possess a leader with the charismatic appeal of a Nenni. Although the mass popularity of Asanuma was sometimes remarked, it is probably fair to say that he only assumed 'charismatic' value after his assassination in 1960. Eda might, perhaps, be thought of in some such terms. His use of television to project his image as a party leader probably helped to consolidate his position, at least for a time. In the end, however, his personal style and his relatively moderate, reformist type of socialism did not save him from defeat by the careful techniques of factional organization combined with doctrinaire ideological appeal of the personally unimpressive Sasaki. Sasaki himself, as party Chairman, had a certain 'proletarian' appeal although this was probably exaggerated by the press.

Nenni, on the other hand, exercised his hold over the mass following of the PSI not only because of his long association with Italian socialism (including long periods as its leader), but also for his reputation as a hero of the anti-fascist resistance during World War II. The importance of the wartime resistance movement for the subsequent history of the Italian Left is hard to overestimate. In contrast, the Japanese Left did not have a similar 'heroic' experience to which it could make reference. Large sections of the movement had, passively or actively, co-operated with the militarists, and those who had not (including especially the communists) had spent the war in prison or in exile, without being able to influence in any way the course of events.

The importance of charisma in the PSI leadership depended in part upon the organization of the party itself. Conversely the lack of success of a similar technique in the JSP depended upon that party's organization. One obvious difference between the two parties lay in their membership figures. Personal membership in the JSP was static at slightly over 50,000. In the PSI, membership reached nearly 500,000.[8] Since neither party relied on a system of bloc trade union membership, such as applied in the British Labour Party, it seems legitimate to compare the membership figures of the two parties without apology.

Mass membership does not necessarily mean mass participation in the decision-making processes of a party. One political scientist, analysing trends in the PSI, has stressed the oligarchic nature of the party even after the return to 'intra-party democracy' in 1956, when the Autonomist factions got the upper hand and connections with the communists were loosened. His argument is that because of the high proportion of 'sleeping members' who do not actively participate in party work, democracy is lost and factions gain control, while national congresses of the party are merely 'a discourse between the leaders'.[9] He admits, however, that in certain circumstances, notably during national election campaigns and at branch congresses, there is wide participation and substantive political issues are discussed.[10]

In the JSP, on the other hand, the oligarchic structure is far more pronounced. Not only has membership not exceeded 60,000, but it is claimed that active members have been no more than 5,000 to 10,000.[11] The party is backed by *Sōhyō*, but few rank and file trade unionists play an active role in party affairs as such. Moreover, whereas the PSI is well entrenched in local administration in many areas of Italy, the JSP has always been conspicuously less successful in local elections (and especially in elections for city, town and village councils) than in the national elections. Here we come upon a fundamental difference between the organization of the JSP and that of our Italian model: However oligarchic the structure of the PSI may have been, it has always possessed (like the PCI) a dedicated grassroots following among the working class, prepared to identify itself with the party as well as to vote for it. Despite the evidence of mass demonstrations to the contrary, the JSP has never enjoyed this advantage to the same extent.

There seem to be two main reasons for this. First, the roots of socialism in Japan have been principally intellectual. Because of persecution and generally unfavourable political conditions, there was little effective socialist mass organization before World War II. The socialist parties which proliferated after 1925 remained little more than intellectual discussion groups, or personal support groups for particular leaders, or both. For the Italian socialist movement, in contrast, the proletarian socialist traditions forged in the late nineteenth and early twentieth centuries, were not difficult to revive by socialist (and communist) leaders once twenty years of suppression had ended.

Second, the Japanese habits of hierarchy and paternalism, inherited from the Tokugawa period and deliberately perpetuated by pre-war governments as a form of national discipline, did not encourage the development of popular movements with active mass participation. The tradition of élitist leadership, whereby a small number of immediate supporters worked for a particular leader, who in turn looked after their interests, encouraged the fragmentation of political parties into factions, at first regionally based, but more recently mainly personal in nature. These operated almost independently of any central party organization that might exist. In the case of the JSP, as also in the conservative parties, many of the faction leaders from the pre-war period resumed their positions after the war or after the end of the Occupation, and continued their pre-war tradition of essentially personal leadership.

Our comparison of the JSP with an important European

socialist party has indicated some of the important differences
of substance underlying apparent similarities of form. Duverger
maintained that the 'branch' was the typical unit of organization of (European) socialist parties and of parties modelling
themselves on socialist forms of organization. He further held
that, despite appearances to the contrary, parties founded upon
branches were more centralized and oligarchic than parties
founded upon what he considered to be the typical unit of
'bourgeois' organization, the 'caucus'.[12] If we attempt to fit the
JSP into Duverger's scheme we strike the paradox that although
the party is founded on branches they are not units of mass
organization (like those in the PSI) but more akin to the can-
didate-support groups typical, according to Duverger, of 'caucus'
parties. In the European context, it seems, a party leadership
that knows what it wants will find it easier to bend a party to
its will if that party is founded on a mass of affiliated supporters
organized into branches, than if the party consists of a relatively
few individuals with interests and patronage of their own.

Both the JSP and the PSI were reft by factionalism. Whereas,
however, the mass organization of the PSI permitted one group
of leaders not only to gain control but also to change the direction of the party in a radical and purposeful manner, attempts
to do the same in the JSP met with limited and temporary
success. JSP leadership is best described in terms of weakness
and its policies in terms of inconsistency, bred of the necessity
of constant compromise between the party's loosely coherent
parts.

The results of the Lower House general election of January
1967 indicate that the party's electoral stagnation of recent years
may be turning into a slow decline.[13] It is very pertinent to ask,
therefore, whether this is primarily a measure of the electorate's
disillusionment with the party's anti-American foreign policy,
which has lately seemed to take a pro-Peking orientation. Would
a more moderate neutralist line, seeking to loosen Japan's ties
with the United States but realistic and pragmatic about Asia
and Japan's role in Asian international relations, appeal to the
electorate more? There is little doubt about the attractiveness
to Japanese public opinion of a more independent foreign policy
than that being currently pursued by the government, while

the strength of pacifism and isolationism, very marked after the war, has probably diminished. Nevertheless it is important to ask whether foreign policy issues, or indeed any policy issues of a general kind, really swing elections in Japan. There is a good deal of evidence that they do not, or at least that they have a far less important effect upon elections than they do in countries such as Australia, Britain or the United States. Public opinion polls amply demonstrate that the popularity of both government and opposition parties is subject to wide fluctuations depending upon their current political behaviour and handling of major policy issues. These fluctuations, however, scarcely affect the results of general elections. Thus according to *Asahi* public opinion polls the popularity of the Kishi government dived from a high point of 42 per cent support in July 1957 to a low of 12 per cent in May 1960 (just after the Bill ratifying the revised Security Treaty had been forced through the Lower House). In November 1964 the supporters of the Satō government were 47 per cent of the total sample, while exactly two years later, during a series of corruption scandals involving government ministers, the figure had dropped to 25 per cent.[14] If one looks, however, at the proportion of voters actually voting for the Liberal-Democratic Party, one finds a very different picture. In November 1960 (admittedly after Kishi's fall and under a new and more popular Prime Minister) the party polled 57.6 per cent of the total vote. In January 1967, with Satō still in power, it polled 48.8 per cent.

Except for the immediate post-war period, when political allegiances were unusually fluid, Japanese general elections have been influenced mainly by long-term trends involving socioeconomic and demographic changes. The most striking such change is the rapid migration of population from the countryside to the cities, which has been accompanied by a gradual decline in the electoral strength of the LDP. Sudden electoral swings, however, dependent upon temporary political or economic factors, have not occurred.

Western observers sometimes ask why the JSP does not put up more than a limited number of candidates at elections, thus ruling itself out from the start as a government party. (Usually more than 70 per cent of its candidates for Lower House elections have been elected.) It is as if the British Labour Party only put up candidates for safe seats. The reason is quite simply that in its electoral behaviour the JSP acts like a traditional Japanese political party. What matters is not the strategy or platform of central headquarters, but the personal support groups built up by individual candidates at the constituency level. In the case of the JSP, the backing and funds to establish and foster these support groups comes mainly from local trade unions and is distributed either through the JSP factions or directly to candidates who are sponsored by the trade unions involved.

This highly particularistic mode of electoral behaviour is characteristic of rural Japan, from which the LDP gets its most solid support. It has been amply demonstrated, however, that typical urban patterns of voting differ substantially from the rural model.[15] Voter loyalties are rather less dependable, less blind, than in the traditional rural areas. One might well suppose, therefore, that the JSP, whose main support is in the big cities and industrial areas, would find it advantageous to adopt a more policy-centred approach, relying less on the ability of individual trade unionists to 'sew up' a particular group of voters. One important difficulty, however, lies in the fact that the tight personal loyalties of the countryside, which lead to very high voter turnouts, are replaced in the big cities not so much by an attention to policies as by voter apathy. This is seen very clearly in a comparison of voting percentages at the Lower House general election of November 1963. Whereas the proportion of those eligible who voted over the country as a whole was 71.1 per cent and in the rural areas taken as a whole was as high as 78.7 per cent, the corresponding percentages for the seven largest cities was as follows: Tokyo, 59.1; Kyōto, 56.9; Ōsaka, 56.9; Nagoya, 56.9; Kita Kyūshū, 65.5; Kōbe, 55.1; Yokohama, 52.5.[16]

These figures suggest a very considerable degree of disinterest in politics in the very areas which might be expected to be Socialist strongholds. It is in these very areas that the mass mobilization techniques of the *Kōmeitō* (Clean Government Party) (the political party formed by the Buddhist sect *Sōka Gakkai* or Value Creation Society), and to a lesser extent the JCP, have had some success in the last few years. These techniques depend less upon personal loyalties to candidates and the material benefits that are thought to result from such loyalties, than upon the attractiveness to the underprivileged and insecure of membership of a mass movement. In all probability the scope for further expansion of these movements is limited by the entrenched position of the LDP and JSP. Nevertheless, their progress is a measure of the failure of the JSP to modify its organization to take account of the changes in voting behaviour brought about by rapid urbanization.

Since, however, the electoral position of the JSP depends to a very great extent on the resources and backing of the *Sōhyō* unions, any major decision to unify electoral strategy would have to gain trade union approval. This would be a tough task indeed. There are recent indications that *Sōhyō* itself is undergoing a crisis of readjustment to changing industrial conditions, from which it may well emerge seriously weakened. This, indeed, may be part of the reason for the latest Socialist electoral decline. The advance of an organization known as the 'International Metal Workers Federation: Japan Chapter' on to the Japanese trade union scene has posed a serious challenge to the hegemony of *Sōhyō*, two thirds of whose affiliated workers belong to unions in state enterprises and the public service. Faced with the possibility of a decline in the cohesion and strength of its established 'base', the JSP may react in ways that are difficult to predict.[17]

None of this, however, suggests that the electoral problem has much to do with extremism or otherwise in the party's foreign policy. The recent slight electoral gains of the DSP are less a victory for 'moderation' than a result of improved organization and in particular the progress that *Dōmei (Zen-Nihon Rōdō Sōdōmei)* (All-Japan Labour Federation), which backs the DSP, has been making at the expense of *Sōhyō*. The DSP may be placed in the same category of particularistic parties as the JSP.

If, therefore, our discussion of JSP foreign policy has been conducted largely at the level of the top leadership echelons it is because at this level foreign policy has always been of major importance. Yet at the level of the local party and trade union organization a leader's pronouncements on foreign policy serve only an incantational purpose, if any purpose at all. Here the real business is that of personality and patronage. At the top level too, the merits of issues are often obscured by factionalism. Factionalism, as we have seen, has a complicated rationale in which (in the JSP at least) ideology and personal advantage interwine. The power situation, and thus the foreign policy line at a particular time, is likely to depend on a number of factors, of which the following are the most important:

First, the ideological view which the faction proposes, and its degree of commitment to that view. Second, personal loyalties and mutual obligations within a process whose main aim is the allocation of party executive posts. Third, the relative strengths of the factions, and their skill in political manoeuvre. Fourth, the ideological position of a faction in relation to that of all other factions. Thus a faction (such as that of Nishio) on the extreme right may find it especially difficult to compromise with factions of the far left.

Essentially, in tracing the fluctuations in the policy of neutralism, we have been charting this continuing process of factional and ideological manoeuvre and adjustment. The policy has also been affected by a host of external factors on the domestic political and international scene, but in the last analysis what the party calls its foreign policy is the outcome of an internal and often temporary factional compromise.

Over the period we have studied, two long-term factors may be noted. One is that at certain times (1960–2 is a good example) the pre-existing factional alliance structure breaks down and a new structure has to be created. This is the period in which genuine innovation is most likely, as new leaders are thrown up. The other factor is that factional identification and distinctiveness on the basis of a common ideology has gradually given way to something much closer to the predominantly personal factionalism of the LDP. This is not to say that the party is no longer interested in ideology, but that ideological differences are no longer quite so important an element in factionalism as they were during the 1950s. For one thing, by the 1960s the intensely ideological pre-war tradition of Japanese socialism was wearing thin, as many of the 'pre-war' leaders disappeared from the scene. For another, the defection of most of the right in 1959–60 meant that the party was in traditional terms nearly all 'left wing'. Conflict between the Structural Reformers and their opponents, though bitter, had a more purely factional character, which has become more marked as time has gone on. This has not eliminated the recurrent tendency of the party to drift to the left in response to real or imagined pressure from left wing militants. We are therefore faced with the paradox of a party capable of the extremes of doctrinaire argument, which behaves on most other levels much like its conservative opponent. A return to the main lines of its neutralist tradition may yet prove the best way for the party to hold its own in a situation where it will have to take increasing account of the views of other political parties.

APPENDIX

A questionnaire was distributed through party channels to all members of the Upper and Lower Houses of the Japanese Diet belonging to the JSP. One distribution was made in December 1962 and another (to those who had not replied) in February 1963. Out of a total of 209 Socialist Diet members, 84 replies (i.e. 40 per cent of the total) were received. Completed questionnaire forms were returned to the writer by post.

The main purpose of the questionnaire was to test opinions formed in the course of study of the party (including personal interviews with its members) about its basic foreign policy orientation. A secondary purpose was to investigate the extent to which foreign policy views corresponded with factional membership. To these ends a series of questions requiring 'check' answers was formulated, followed by a number of 'open-ended' questions permitting the respondent to state his views at length. In order to collate replies with factional allegiance, the respondent's identity was first ascertained by means of a number on each questionnaire form, and a recent factional membership list of all Diet members (received privately) was then used to ascribe respondents to factions. It is not claimed that the analysis of replies according to factions represents a high degree of accuracy, for two reasons: first, the factional allegiance of many Diet members is vague and shifting. The factional list employed gave a number of Diet members as strictly belonging to no faction, but with a leaning towards a particular faction. In the tabulation of results these have been ascribed to the faction in question, but enclosed in brackets. The list also represented a few members as belonging to one faction, but as also having a certain leaning towards another faction. These have been ascribed without qualification to the first.

Second, the proportion of replies received per faction to the total number of Diet members said to belong to that faction differed widely; thus the proportion, expressed as a percentage (those with vague ascriptions included), was as follows:

	Replies received	Percentage of total membership
Heiwa Dōshikai	4	24
Nomizo	1	17
Sasaki	19 (3)	45
Eda	4 (4)	26
Wada	32	54
Kawakami	12 (1)	35

One striking characteristic of the replies to the questionnaire was the extremely high consensus of opinion among respondents on several questions, contrasted with the wide variety of opinion among them on others (especially those that were 'open-ended').

Respondents were in substantial agreement on the desirability of neutralization and lack of danger associated with it, and in their fear of the nuclear arms race and nuclear testing. 92 per cent thought that the nuclear arms race between eastern and western camps was 'a very big threat' (4Aa); 92 per cent thought Soviet resumption of nuclear testing in 1961 was 'completely impermissible' (5b); 95 per cent thought that Japan's neutralization was 'necessary' (8A); 84 per cent thought that if Japan became neutralist there would be no danger to her security (9A)—of the minority which admitted any danger, only two mentioned 'measures of self-defence' as a way of coping with the danger; 88 per cent thought that if Japan became neutralist there would be no fear of upsetting the balance of power and thus endangering world peace (10).

On the other hand, when asked about the prospects for a neutralist Japan, and when invited to write down what was the nature and purpose of, and conditions for, neutralism in Japan (8B-E), respondents gave a variety of answers. There was rather more concern with the implications of a neutralist policy for Japan than with its possible contribution to world peace. Abolition of the Security Treaty, removal of military bases and freedom from military alliances (the aims for which the party had long campaigned) figured largely among the former. Also their relative evaluation of the United States, the Soviet Union and communist China (4Ab-d and 11) was far from unanimous, although American policies were attacked much more readily than Soviet or Chinese.

The replies did not indicate any obvious factional alignments on any of the questions asked, with the exception of Question 6 on Structural Reform. Here of the pro-Structural Reform factions (Eda, Wada and Kawakami) 34 out of 40 respondents (i.e. 85 per cent) supported Structural Reform, while of the anti-Structural Reform factions (*Heiwa Dōshikai*, Nomizo and Sasaki) 14 out of 23 (i.e. 61 per cent) opposed Structural Reform. From this it may be concluded that Structural Reform played a more important part in the factional struggle, so far as Diet members as a whole were concerned, than matters of foreign policy. This would suggest that at least in the transitional factional situation of 1962–3 differences of opinion on foreign policy occurred to a considerable extent independently of factional membership, although the factional leaders undoubtedly used foreign policy issues as counters in factional struggles. (The number of replies from *Heiwa Dōshikai*, whose ideology significantly differed from that of the other factions, was too small to permit generalization.)

RESULTS OF QUESTIONNAIRE

Question 1. From the present standpoint of the JSP, do you think that domestic problems or international problems are the more important?
   (a) Domestic problems   (b) International problems
   (c) Cannot say

	H.D.*	Nomizo	Sasaki	Eda	Wada	Kawakami	Unclassified	Total
(a)	0	0	3 (1)	1 (1)	8	3	0	17
(b)	1	0	7	0 (2)	9	4	1	24
(c)	3	0	9 (2)	2	14	4 (1)	3	35
Other replies	0	1	0	1 (1)	1	1	0	5
							Total	84

Question 2. Are you personally more interested in domestic problems or international problems?
   (a) Domestic problems   (b) International problems
   (c) Cannot say

* H.D. = *Heiwa Dōshikai*.

	H.D.	Nomizo	Sasaki	Eda	Wada	Kawakami	Unclassi-fied	Total
(a)	0	0	6 (1)	1 (2)	14	5	2	31
(b)	1	0	4	0	9	2	1	17
(c)	3	1	9 (2)	2 (1)	8	4 (1)	1	32
Other	0	0	0	1 (1)	1	1	0	4

Total 84

Question 3. By what means do you usually obtain knowledge about international problems? Of the ways listed below please mark the one(s) you mainly use. If you use any other methods, please mention them under 'Others'.

No. of respondents

(a)	Party reports	39
(b)	Foreign materials collected yourself	29
(c)	Careful reading of foreign news in Japanese newspapers	69
(d)	Listening to what people say	23
(e)	Others	22

Those who wrote in a supplementary answer under (e) claimed to broaden their knowledge of international events from the following sources:

No. of respondents

(i)	English magazines	1
(ii)	Government and Foreign Office materials	4
(iii)	Japanese magazines	4
(iv)	Materials of the Diet Foreign Policy Committee	1
(v)	Materials obtained through organizations outside the Party	2
(vi)	Materials sent from abroad	2
(vii)	Meeting foreigners	1
(viii)	National Diet Library	2
(ix)	Visits abroad	3

Question 4A. Do you think that the following things have presented a threat to peace? To what extent do you think that they have presented a threat?

(a) The nuclear arms race between eastern and western camps.

(i) A very big threat (ii) A considerable threat
(iii) A small threat (iv) No threat
(v) Don't know

	H.D.	Nomizo	Sasaki	Eda	Wada	Kawakami	Unclassi-fied	Total
(i)	3	1	18 (3)	3 (4)	30	10 (1)	4	77
(ii)	0	0	1	1	2	2	0	6
(iii)	0	0	0	0	0	0	0	0
(iv)	0	0	0	0	0	0	0	0
(v)	0	0	0	0	0	0	0	0
No reply	1	0	0	0	0	0	0	1

Total 84

(b) The recent world policies of the United States.
 (i) A very big threat   (ii) A considerable threat
(iii) A small threat   (iv) No threat
 (v) Don't know

	H.D.	Nomizo	Sasaki	Eda	Wada	Kawakami	Unclassi-fied	Total
(i)	4	0	12 (3)	2 (3)	22	5 (1)	3	55
(ii)	0	1	5	1	8	4	0	19
(iii)	0	0	0	1	1	2	1	5
(iv)	0	0	0	0	0	1	0	1
(v)	0	0	0	0	1	0	0	1
Other	0	0	2	1	0	0	0	3

Total   84

(c) The recent world policies of the Soviet Union.
 (i) A very big threat   (ii) A considerable threat
(iii) A small threat   (iv) No threat
 (v) Don't know

	H.D.	Nomizo	Sasaki	Eda	Wada	Kawakami	Unclassi-fied	Total
(i)	0	0	4 (1)	0 (2)	9	1 (1)	1	19
(ii)	0	1	7 (1)	2	7	3	0	21
(iii)	2	0	5 (1)	1 (1)	6	3	1	20
(iv)	1	0	1	1	9	4	2	18
(v)	0	0	0	0	1	0	0	1
Other replies/no reply	1	0	2	0 (1)	0	1	0	5

Total   84

(d) The recent world policies of the Chinese Peoples' Republic.
 (i) A very big threat   (ii) A considerable threat
(iii) A small threat   (iv) No threat
 (v) Don't know

	H.D.	Nomizo	Sasaki	Eda	Wada	Kawakami	Unclassi-fied	Total
(i)	0	0	5	0 (1)	3	3 (1)	0	13
(ii)	0	0	5 (3)	0 (1)	10	5	0	24
(iii)	0	1	2	2 (1)	9	2	3	20
(iv)	3	0	5	1	7	1	1	18
(v)	0	0	1	0	1	0	0	2
Other replies/no reply	1	0	1	1 (1)	2	1	0	7

Total   84

Question 4B. Of (a), (b), (c), (d) above, which do you think presents the greatest danger to world peace? Please write one only.

	H.D.	Nomizo	Sasaki	Eda	Wada	Kawakami	Unclassi- fied	Total
(a)	1	0	9 (1)	2 (4)	19	6 (1)	4	47
(b)	2	0	6	2	8	2	0	20
(c)	0	0	0	0	0	0	0	0
(d)	0	0	2	0	1	0	0	3
Other	0	1	1	0	2	1	0	5
No reply	1	0	1 (2)	0	2	3	0	9

Total 84

Question 5. In the international situation of the time, do you think that the following actions of the United States and of the Soviet Union were justified, unavoidable, or completely impermissible?
(a) The Soviet resumption of nuclear testing on 1 September 1961.
(i) Justified (ii) Unavoidable (iii) Completely impermissible

	H.D.	Nomizo	Sasaki	Eda	Wada	Kawakami	Unclassi- fied	Total
(i)	0	0	0	0	0	0	0	0
(ii)	0	0	1	1	1	0	2	5
(iii)	4	1	18 (3)	3 (3)	30	12 (1)	2	77
Other	0	0	0	0 (1)	1	0	0	2

Total 84

(b) The American resumption of nuclear testing on 15 September 1961.
(i) Justified (ii) Unavoidable (iii) Completely impermissible

	H.D.	Nomizo	Sasaki	Eda	Wada	Kawakami	Unclassi- fied	Total
(i)	0	0	0	0	0	0	0	0
(ii)	0	0	1	1	0	0	0	2
(iii)	4	1	18 (3)	3 (3)	31	12 (1)	4	80
Other	0	0	0	0 (1)	1	0	0	2

Total 84

Question 6. Do you support Structural Reform?
(a) Support (b) Not support (c) Not yet decided

Appendix

	H.D.	Nomizo	Sasaki	Eda	Wada	Kawakami	Unclassi-fied	Total
(a)	1	0	6 (2)	3 (4)	24	12 (1)	3	56
(b)	3	1	9 (1)	0	6	0	1	21
(c)	0	0	1	0	2	0	0	3
Other	0	0	3	1	0	0	0	4

Total 84

Question 7. In the process of revolution envisaged by the JSP, do you attach primary importance to a struggle against Japanese monopoly capital; or do you attach primary importance to liberation from American monopoly capital, and think that only after that will it be possible to achieve a domestic socialist revolution? Please indicate briefly what you think on this issue.

The replies to this question were classified under the following heads, depending on the relative emphasis given to the 'struggle' against Japanese capitalists and to the anti-American 'struggle':
  (a) Precedence to former (unqualified)
  (b) Precedence to former (qualified by some emphasis on latter)
  (c) Precedence to neither
  (d) Precedence to latter (qualified by some emphasis on former)
  (e) Precedence to latter (unqualified)

	H.D.	Nomizo	Sasaki	Eda	Wada	Kawakami	Unclassi-fied	Total
(a)	2	1	7	1 (1)	20	5 (1)	1	39
(b)	2	0	3	2 (1)	5	5	1	19
(c)	0	0	6	1 (1)	4	1	0	13
(d)	0	0	1 (1)	0	1	0	0	3
(e)	0	0	1	0 (1)	2	0	1	5
Other	0	0	1	0	0	0	1	2
No reply	0	0	0 (2)	0	0	1	0	3

Total 84

Question 8A. I should now like to turn to the question of neutralism. Do you think that Japan's neutralization is necessary or not necessary?
  (a) Necessary   (b) Not necessary   (c) Don't know
  (d) Others (please specify)

H.D.	Nomizo	Sasaki	Eda	Wada	Kawakami	Unclassi-fied	Total
(a)	4	1	19 (3)	4 (4)	30	12 (1)	4	82
(b)	0	0	0	0	1	0	0	1
(c)	0	0	0	0	0	0	0	0
(d)	0	0	0	0	1	0	0	1

Total 84

Question 8B. Do you think that there is a prospect of bringing about the neutralization of Japan in the next few years or not? (a) Yes (b) No (c) Don't know (d) Others (please specify)

H.D.	Nomizo	Sasaki	Eda	Wada	Kawakami	Unclassi-fied	Total
(a)	4	1	10 (3)	1 (1)	19	6 (1)	1	47
(b)	0	0	3	0 (2)	7	3	1	16
(c)	0	0	1	1	1	2	2	7
(d)	0	0	5	2 (1)	5	1	0	14

Total 84

Those who wrote in supplementary answers made the following points:

No. of respondents

(i) The achievement of neutralism for Japan will be difficult and requires determination — 8
(ii) Prospects for neutralism in Japan depend on the JSP attaining power — 6
(iii) Prospects for neutralism in Japan will brighten when the term of the present Security Treaty comes to an end (i.e. 1970) — 3
(iv) Prospects for neutralism in Japan depend on the relaxation of international tension — 2

Question 8C. If Japan became neutralist, what kind of neutralism would you hope for? Please indicate briefly what you think on this question.

The replies to this section were divided into two categories: those stressing the 'positive' international aspects of the policy, and those concentrating on its implications for Japan—especially in so far as was thought to concern her security, independence and national advantage. In addition to the types of reply listed below, sixteen respondents mentioned the official JSP name of the policy—'positive neutrality'—in place of or in addition to a description of its content. Most respondents gave more than one facet or implication of the policy.

Replies stressing the 'positive' international aspects of neutralism:

		No. of respondents
(a)	Contribution to world disarmament	4
(b)	Strengthening of the United Nations	4
(c)	Promotion of neutralism abroad	4
(d)	Contribution to world peace	3
(e)	Establishment of a non-nuclear zone in the Far East	3
(f)	Dissolution of military blocs	2
(g)	Promotion of peaceful co-existence	2
(h)	Contribution to world federation	1

Replies concentrating on the implications of neutralism for Japan:

		No. of respondents
(a)	No military alliances with any country	19
(b)	A 'Locarno-type' treaty of non-aggression between Japan, the United States, the Soviet Union and China	12
(c)	Independence (especially from the United States and the Soviet Union) and independent judgment in international affairs	11
(d)	Relations (especially economic and cultural) equally with both sides in the cold war	10
(e)	Abolition of the Security Treaty and withdrawal of military bases from Japan	8
(f)	Neutralism as the implementation of the 'Pacifist Clause' of the Constitution	7
(g)	*Unarmed* neutralism	6
(h)	A United Nations guarantee of Japanese security	4
(i)	Peace Treaties with the Soviet Union and China	3
(j)	Neutralism as a means of protecting Japan from annihilation in war	1
(k)	Abolition of the Sino-Soviet Treaty	1
(l)	Neutralism to increase Japan's international standing in the United Nations	1
(m)	Neutralism to strengthen ties with neutralist nations	1
(n)	Neutralism as a means of making the United States and Soviet Union recognize Japan economically and politically as an equal	1

Question 8D. If Japan were to become a neutralist country under a socialist government, what sort of role do you think she would be able to play in international questions? Please indicate briefly what you think on this question.

Replies to this section were divided into the following categories:

		No. of respondents
(a)	Relaxation of the east-west conflict and international tension, achievement of peaceful co-existence	26
(b)	World disarmament (including nuclear disarmament)	16
(c)	Japan to have the role of a mediator (or 'bridge') in the cold war	13
(d)	Japan to have a leading role in the development of under-developed countries	4
(e)	Restoration of diplomatic relations with China	2
(f)	Strengthening of the United Nations	2
(g)	Contribution to world federation	2
(h)	Economic co-operation	2
(i)	The amendment of American policies	1

Question 8E. Irrespective of whether you support it or not, what conditions do you consider necessary for the speedy realization of Japan's neutralism? Please indicate briefly what you think on this question.

Replies to this question were divided into the following categories:

		No. of respondents
(a)	Abolition of the Security Treaty	39
(b)	Establishment of a socialist government in Japan	22
(c)	Reversion of Okinawa to Japan	9
(d)	Closer relations with the Soviet Union and communist China	8
(e)	Affirmation of peaceful co-existence by the United States and the Soviet Union	8
(f)	Abolition of the anti-Japanese clause in the Sino-Soviet Treaty	7
(g)	Reduction of the Self-Defence Forces and defence of the Constitution	7
(h)	Disarmament (including nuclear disarmament)	5
(i)	The independence of Japan	4
(j)	Establishment of a non-nuclear zone	3

		No. of respondents
(k)	Reversion to Japan of Habomai and Shikotan*	3
(l)	Establishment of a 'Locarno-type' treaty of non-aggression between Japan, the United States, the Soviet Union and China	3
(m)	Strengthening of world neutralism	2
(n)	Closer relations with North Korea and North Vietnam†	2
(o)	Ending of negotiations with South Korea	1
(p)	Communist China and the Soviet Union to become more powerful	1
(q)	A United Nations guarantee for Japan's security	1
(r)	Communist Chinese membership of the United Nations	1
(s)	Democracy in Japan	1
(t)	Prosperity in Japan	1

Question 9A. If Japan became neutralist, do you think there would be a danger of the security of the state being threatened?
(a) There would be a danger (b) There would be no danger
(c) Don't know (d) Others (please specify)

	H.D.	Nomizo	Sasaki	Eda	Wada	Kawakami	Unclassified	Total
(a)	0	0	0	0	1	1	0	2
(b)	3	1	18 (2)	3 (3)	28	9 (1)	3	71
(c)	1	0	1	0	1	0	1	4
(d)	0	0	0	1	1	2	0	4
No reply	0	0	0 (1)	0 (1)	1	0	0	3
							Total	84

* These respondents also wanted the reversion of Okinawa.
† These respondents also wanted closer relations with the Soviet Union and communist China.

Of those who wrote supplementary answers to this question, five admitted or implied the existence of some minimal degree of danger if Japan became neutralist, while one said that a policy of alliance was a greater danger, and two denied any danger, mentioning the JSP plan for a 'Locarno' settlement in the Far East as sufficient guarantee of security.

Question 9B. If there is such a danger, what policies do you think should be undertaken to deal with it?

		No. of respondents
(a)	No reply	54
(b)	Replied	30

The thirty replies to this question were classified as follows:

(a) Replies rejecting the premise of the question

		No. of respondents
(i)	Aggression not to be expected	7
(ii)	Neutralism essential for security	1
(iii)	Neutralism essential for security, but if there were a war, Japan would be quite impossible to defend	1

(b) Replies accepting the premise of the question

		No. of respondents
(i)	Strengthen the United Nations	5
(ii)	A 'Locarno-type' treaty	4
(iii)	Support (and thus obtain the support of) world opinion (which is naturally pacifist)	3
(iv)	Abolish the Security Treaty and withdraw American military bases	2
(v)	Measures of self-defence	2
(vi)	Domestic stability, prosperity, democracy	2
(vii)	Negotiations	2
(viii)	A non-nuclear zone in the Far East	1
(ix)	Disarmament	1
(x)	Friendly relations with North Korea (since Korea is the only possible source of aggression against Japan)	1
(xi)	Persuade the United States to recognize communist China	1
(xii)	Spread neutralist, pacifist thought	1
(xiii)	World federation	1

Question 10. If Japan became a neutralist country, do you think that there would be any fear of upsetting the balance of power and thus endangering world peace?

(a) Yes (b) No (c) Cannot say (d) Others (please specify)

	H.D.	*Nomizo*	*Sasaki*	*Eda*	*Wada*	*Kawakami*	*Unclassified*	*Total*
(a)	0	0	0	0	0	0	0	0
(b)	4	1	16 (2)	4 (4)	30	9 (1)	3	74
(c)	0	0	2	0	0	1	1	4
(d)	0	0	1 (1)	0	1	2	0	5
No reply	0	0	0	0	1	0	0	1

Total	84

Of those who wrote supplementary answers to this question, two admitted that there might be some slight danger of upsetting the balance of power, five implied that there was no such danger or that it was less than the danger to Japan from a policy of alliance, and one denied the validity of the concept of an east-west power balance as a factor maintaining peace.

Question 11. Not only from the political aspect, but also from the point of view of general feeling, do you prefer the Soviet Union or the United States?
(a) Soviet Union (b) United States (c) Cannot say

	H.D.	Nomizo	Sasaki	Eda	Wada	Kawakami	Unclassified	Total
(a)	1	0	2 (1)	0 (1)	5	0	1	11
(b)	0	0	2	0 (1)	3	3	0	9
(c)	1	1	10 (1)	3 (2)	18	5 (1)	3	45
Other	2	0	5	1	4	4	0	16
No reply	0	0	0 (1)	0	2	0	0	3

Total 84

The supplementary replies to this question were classified as follows:

No. of respondents

(a)	Like both	3
(b)	Like neither	2
(c)	Like neither, but prefer the Soviet Union	1
(d)	Neither like nor dislike either	1
(e)	Like the people but not the policies of both	2
(f)	Like the people but not the policies of the United States	4
(g)	Like the people but not the policies of the Soviet Union	1
(h)	Like the United States because of personal contacts (no mention of policies)	2
(i)	Like American democracy	2
(j)	Dislike Anglo-Saxon racial prejudice and sense of superiority	1
(k)	Like Soviet social security and governmental initiative	1
(l)	Like the Soviet Union for cultural reasons (classical Russian literature)	1
(m)	Like the Soviet Union much better under Krushchev than under Stalin	4
(n)	The question of liking or disliking is irrelevant to the problem of peace	1
(o)	Prefer England to either	1
(p)	Do not fully understand the question	1

NOTES

(All Japanese-language publications are published in Tokyo)

I NEUTRALISM: THE WORLD SETTING AND JAPAN

[1] The results, compared with those of the previous Lower House election (November 1963), were as follows:
(A = 1967 election; B = 1963 election; 1 = distribution of seats; 2 = percentage of total vote.)

	A1	A2	B1	B2
Liberal-Democrats	277	48.8	283	54.7
Socialists	140	27.9	144	29.0
Democratic-Socialists	30	7.4	23	7.4
Kōmeitō	25	5.4	0*	0*
Communists	5	4.8	5	4.0
Other parties	0	0.2	0	0.1
Independents	9	5.5	12	4.8
Total	486	100.0	467	100.0

*Did not stand.

[2] For a stimulating discussion of possible future trends, see H. Passin (ed.), *The United States and Japan*, pp. 141–61.

[3] I. I. Morris, 'Japanese Foreign Policy and Neutralism', *International Affairs*, January 1960, pp. 7–20.

[4] One pre-war champion of the League contemptuously dismissed neutrality as 'destined to disappear'; in N. Politis, *La Neutralité et la Paix* (Paris, 1935), p. 7. See also P. C. Jessup, *Neutrality, its History, Economics and Law*, especially vol. 4.

[5] H. Morgenthau, *Dilemmas of Politics*, pp. 185–209.

[6] See H. Lauterpacht (ed.), *Oppenheim's International Law* (London, 5th ed., 1935), vol. 2, pp. 539–51.

[7] See Morgenthau, op. cit., p. 192.

[8] G. Cohn, *Neo-Neutrality*, p. 21. See also E. Bonjour, *Swiss Neutrality, its History and Meaning*, pp. 137–41.

[9] See especially *Jawaharlal Nehru's Speeches 1949–1953* (New Delhi, 1954), pp. 151–8.

[10] P. Lyon, *Neutralism*, p. 72.

[11] See R. A. Scalapino, ' "Neutralism" in Asia', *American Political Science Review*, vol. 48, no. 1, 1954, pp. 49–62. For a more recent analysis, see J. D. B. Miller, *The Politics of the Third World*.

[12] See Bonjour, op. cit., pp. 121–2.

[13] See an interview with the Indian Socialist leader Lohia during a visit he paid to Japan, reported in *Shakai Shimbun*, 10 September 1951.

[14] L. Beaton and J. Maddox, *The Spread of Nuclear Weapons* (London, 1962), p. 160.

15 See D. H. Mendel, *The Japanese People and Foreign Policy: a Study of Public Opinion in Post-Treaty Japan*, p. 50.
16 H. Passin, 'The Sources of Protest in Japan', *American Political Science Review*, vol. 56, no. 2, 1962, p. 395.
17 'Seinen yo! Jū wo toru na!' It is impossible to convey the sense so concisely in English.
18 For an early example of this oft-recurring theme, see Sakisaka Itsurō, 'Nihon no saigumbi wo meguru shomondai', *Jōhō Tsūshin*, 15 March 1951, pp. 11–22.
19 For one among many examples, see Tsunetō Kyō, 'Sensō hōki no mondai, jō', *Sekai*, May 1949, pp. 14–22.
20 Much valuable material on Socialist attitudes to the Japan-Soviet negotiations of 1955–6 is contained in D. C. Hellmann, 'Japanese Foreign Policy and Domestic Politics: The Peace Agreement with the Soviet Union' (unpubl. Ph.D. thesis, University of California, Berkeley, 1964).
21 The most comprehensive statement of Japanese Socialist policies and views on neutralism (now, however, somewhat dated) is to be found in Yamaguchi Fusao, *Chūritsu, kono minzoku no kadai*. For a sympathetic view from outside the JSP, see Maeshiba Kakuzō and Yamate Haruyuki (eds), *Chūritsu wa jitsugen dekiru ka*. This issue is exhaustively discussed by a group of academics of various viewpoints in *Chūritsushugi no kenkyū*.
22 Sakamoto Yoshikazu, 'Chūritsu Nihon no bōei kōsō: Nichi-Bei ampo taisei ni kawaru mono', *Sekai*, August 1959, pp. 31–47.
23 See, e.g., 'Bei-So sen ga hajimareba', *Nihon Shakai Shimbun*, 15 August 1960.
24 Alleged Chinese and Soviet fears of resurgent Japanese militarism have also (though decreasingly) been used by Japanese Socialists to back up this argument. See, e.g., Yamaguchi, op. cit., pp. 209–10.
25 In March 1966 Prime Minister Satō expressed the opinion that some positive action would have to be taken in or after 1970 to put the Treaty on a more permanent basis. See *Asahi*, 8 March 1966.
26 See however Nishimura Eiichi, 'Tai-Nichi kōwa to waga tō no rekishiteki shimei' (mimeo, [probably mid-1951]). The most famous Japanese exponent of armed neutrality was a radical right wing nationalist, Tsuji Masanobu, the conqueror of Singapore; see his *Jiei chūritsu* (Atō Shobō, 1952).

2 THE JSP AND ITS LEGACY FROM THE PAST

1 See G. O. Totten, 'Problems of Japanese Socialist Leadership', *Pacific Affairs*, June 1955, pp. 160-9. For an extended treatment of socialist movements in Japan up to World War II, see G. O. Totten, *The Social Democratic Movement in Prewar Japan*.
2 The *Rōdō Nōmintō*, formed in 1926 after the grant of manhood suffrage, rapidly disintegrated into four rival parties: the *Shakai Minshūtō* (right), the *Nihon Rōnōtō* (centre) and the *Rōdō Nōmintō* (left). (The fourth was of little importance.) Thus began a kaleidoscopic series of splits and amalgamations, which ended in 1932 with the formation of the *Shakai Taishūtō*, embracing nearly all the main groups. Nevertheless, the group loyalties of the initial split of 1926 persisted long after later events had been forgotten. See Kōno Mitsu, *Nihon shakai seitō shi*.
3 The best source for socialist thought in this period is the *Heimin Shimbun* (Commoners' Newspaper). See Hayashi Shigeru and Nishida Chōjū (eds), *Heimin Shimbun ronsetsu shū* (Iwanami Shoten, 1961).
4 The platforms of the various parties are given in Kōno, op. cit., pp. 54–127.
5 See Shisō no Kagaku Kenkyūkai, *Tenkō* (Heibonsha, 1960), vol. 2, pp. 369–432.

6 For a description of Yamakawa's career, see ibid. He died in 1958.
7 This was the line put forward in the 'Bukharin Thesis' presented by the Comintern to its Japanese disciples on the occasion of the founding of their Communist Party in 1922. Quoted in Shakai Keizai Rōdō Kenkyūjo, *Nihon minshu kakumei ronsō shi* (Itō Shoten, 1947), pp. 9–10 (hereafter called *Ronsō shi*). The 'Bukharin Thesis' was attacked at the time by some Japanese Communists on the grounds that it used the Russian revolutions of 1917 as a model without taking account of Japanese conditions, and especially for its implicit equation of Emperor with Tsar. See *Tenkō*, vol. 2, p. 383; *Ronsō shi*, p. 21. Not all later analyses by the Comintern confirmed that of 1922. The '1931 Thesis', for instance, drew close to the position of the *Rōnō-ha*. See *Ronsō shi*, pp. 88–92.
8 Yamakawa maintained that 'feudal elements' had become effectively subordinated to the bourgeoisie. The bourgeoisie, he argued, had enacted manhood suffrage in 1925 in order more easily to put society under its control. See *Ronsō shi*, pp. 22–3.
9 For the retrospective views of both sides, see Nishio Suehiro, *Taishū to tomo ni: watakushi no hansei no kiroku* (Sekaisha, 1951), pp. 319–52, and Kōno, op. cit., pp. 156–70.
10 The source which has been mainly followed in this account of Akamatsu and Asō is *Tenkō* (Heibonsha, 1959), vol. 1, pp. 69–113.
11 Ibid., p. 90.
12 Ibid.
13 Akamatsu Katsumaro, *Nihon shakai undō shi*, p. 288. For comment, see Tanaka Sōgorō, *Yoshino Sakuzō* (Miraisha, 1958), p. 385.
14 At this period Asō wrote a number of novels reminiscent of Russian populism.
15 The present writer owes this interpretation to Kawakami Tamio (son of the late Kawakami Jōtarō who was Asō's close associate in the 1930s and later became Chairman of the JSP), interviewed 13 March 1963.
16 *Tenkō*, vol. 1, p. 111.
17 Kōno, op. cit., p. 132.
18 See, e.g., *Tenkō*, vol. 1, p. 111.
19 For confirmation of this point, see ibid., p. 96.
20 Interview with Kawakami Tamio, 13 March 1963.
21 Kōno, op. cit., p. 148.

3 THE JSP ADOPTS 'PERMANENT NEUTRALITY'

1 Quoted in *Shakai Shimbun*, 10 December 1949.
2 See *Kampō* (*gōgai*), 8 April 1949, pp. 146–51.
3 The principal manifestos of this group were assembled in a supplement to *Sekai*, September 1962, pp. 10–60.
4 *Asahi*, 12 February 1949.
5 Ibid., 14 February 1949.
6 *Daily Mail* (London), 2 March 1949.
7 *New York Times*, 5 November 1949.
8 Quoted in Yamazaki Hiroshi, *Nihon Shakaitō no jūnen shi*, p. 19.
9 See *Teikoku kempō kaisei shingiroku, sensō hōki hen* (Sangiin Jimukyoku, 1952), pp. 91–4.
10 See, e.g., Nihon Shakaitō Seimu Chōsakai oyobi Senkyo Iinkai, *Nihon Shakaitō seisaku shishin* (1948), pp. 9–13; Nihon Shakaitō Kyōikubu, *Nihon Shakaitō kyōiku tekisuto* (Daichi Shuppansha, 1947), pp. 5–7.
11 *Teikoku kempō kaisei shingiroku, sensō hōki hen*, pp. 38–40, 50–3.
12 *Shakai Shimbun*, 30 October 1949.

13 Nishio himself was allegedly involved in these scandals, and was expelled from the party.

14 Factional disharmony brought about a complete three-way split between the three factions lasting from January to April 1950. Foreign policy, however, was scarcely involved.

15 See the comments of a member of the Nishio faction, Hatano Kanae, quoted in *Shakai Shimbun*, 25 November 1949.

16 Yoshida Shigeru, *The Yoshida Memoirs* (London, 1961), p. 265.

17 Sakisaka Itsurō, 'Heiwa wo habamu mono', *Shakai Shimbun*, 18 August 1949.

18 *Shakai Shimbun*, 30 October 1949.

4 THE GREAT SPLIT

1 Quoted in *Nihon Rōdō Nenkan*, 1952, p. 690.

2 *Yomiuri*, 29 July 1950.

3 For an account of the rise and decline of communist influence in the trade union movement, the measures taken to combat it by means of 'Democratization Leagues', and the founding of *Sōhyō* after eighteen months of difficult negotiation, see S. B. Levine, *Industrial Relations in Postwar Japan*, pp. 66–77.

4 See *Sōhyō*, 5 August 1950, p. 31; 15 August 1950, p. 76.

5 Quoted in *Nihon Rōdō Nenkan*, 1952, p. 691.

6 *Nippon Times*, 1 January 1951.

7 Quoted in Yanada Kōki, *Nihon Shakaitō*, p. 76.

8 Quoted in *Nihon Rōdō Nenkan*, 1953, pp. 544–5.

9 Ibid., pp. 545–9.

10 Quoted in *Sōhyō*, 15 March 1950, p. 76.

11 Ibid., 15 July 1950, p. 26.

12 See ibid., 5 December 1950, p. 55.

13 See *Asahi*, 29 November 1950. For the foreign policy views of this group of unions, see *Tōkyō*, 13 August 1950.

14 For Hosoya's views, see *Shakai Shimbun*, 25 August 1950.

15 See *Asahi*, 10 and 11 March 1951.

16 See *Sōhyō*, 5 December 1950, p. 55.

17 *Yomiuri*, 31 May 1951.

18 Ibid. (evening edn), 18 July 1951.

19 This account is largely taken from 'Chūō iinkai ni teiji sareta kōwa mondai ni taisuru shiryō', in 'Dai 8 kai (rinji) taikai hōkokusho' (mimeo, Nihon Shakaitō, 3 October 1951), part 2, pp. 1–22.

20 For a different view, implying armed neutrality, put forward by one leading member of the Nishio faction, see Nishimura Eiichi, 'Tai-Nichi kōwa to waga tō no rekishiteki shimei' (mimeo, [probably mid-1951]).

21 See Yamazaki Hiroshi, *Nihon Shakaitō no jūnen shi*, pp. 97–102; Sasada Shigeru, *Nihon Shakaitō*, vol. 1, pp. 138–9.

22 A minority in an intellectual study group close to the Suzuki faction at this time supported the idea of a 'people's militia'. See *Shakai Shimbun*, 10 February 1951. For a refutation of this position, see Sakisaka Itsurō, 'Nihon no saigumbi wo meguru shomondai', *Jōhō Tsūshin*, 15 March 1951, pp. 11–22.

5 NEUTRALISM AND 'SOCIAL DEMOCRACY'

1 Text in *Nihon Rōdō Nenkan*, 1954, pp. 679–81.

2 In *Yomiuri*, 31 January 1952.

3 See Suzuki Mosaburō, *et al.*, 'Dai 8 kai Komisuko Sōkai narabini dai 1 kai Shakaishugi Intanashionaru taikai ni kansuru hōkokusho' (mimeo, Nihon Shakaitō, [probably August 1951]); Yamazaki Hiroshi, *Nihon Shakaitō no jūnen shi*, pp. 126–7.

4 See Nihon Shakaitō Chūō Shikkō Iinkai, '1953 nendo Nihon Shakaitō undō hōshin (an)', (mimeo, January 1953); Itō Kōdō, 'Heiwa wo motomeru issai no seiryoku', *Shakai Taimusu*, 22 January 1953.

5 See Preparatory Committee, ASC, *Report of Preliminary Meeting for the Asian Socialist Conference* (Rangoon, March 1952).

6 See ASC, *Reports of Sub-Committees 'A', 'B' and 'C'*, *Asian Socialist Conference* (Rangoon, January 1953).

7 See *Shakai Taimusu*, 22 January 1953.

8 See, e.g., ibid., 1 March 1953.

9 See, e.g., *Report of Preliminary Meeting for the Asian Socialist Conference*, p. 83.

10 See public opinion polls quoted in D. H. Mendel, *The Japanese People and Foreign Policy*, p. 102.

11 Texts in *Nihon Rōdō Nenkan*, 1954, pp. 675–81.

12 *1953 nendo Nihon Shakaitō undō hōshin (an)*, pp. 1–2.

13 For a contemporary criticism of neutralism from a *Kōza-ha* standpoint, see Okakura Koshirō, *Dai san seiryoku, chūritsu to heiwa*.

14 *1953 nendo Nihon Shakaitō undō hōshin (an)*, p. 5.

15 For official comment see *Sōhyō*, 25 July 1952, p. 213.

16 For text of the Action Policy, see *Shakaishugi (gōgai)*, July 1954, pp. 19–24. Takano's remarks at the Congress are reported in *Sōhyō*, 19 July 1953, p. 310.

17 *Sōhyō*, 17 July 1953, p. 309.

18 See *Asahi*, 10 July 1953.

19 *Sōhyō*, 17 July 1953, p. 309.

20 See, e.g., Katsumata Seiichi, in *Shakai Taimusu*, 1 March 1953.

21 See, e.g., Tsuru Shigeto, 'MSA to Nihon', *Sekai*, August 1953, pp. 18–27.

22 Interview with Hosoya Matsuta, 22 April 1963.

23 Interviews with Okada Sōji, 18 October 1962; Ōuchi Hyōei, 12 December 1962; Hosoya Matsuta, 22 April 1963.

24 See *Shakai Taimusu*, 19 July 1953.

25 Controversies surrounding the setting up of the committee are discussed in *Asahi* (evening edn), 22 January 1953.

26 Quoted in *Nihon Rōdō Nenkan*, 1955, pp. 746–54.

27 See 'Nihon Shakaitō kōryō kaisetsu shiryō' (mimeo, Nihon Shakaitō, November 1953), pp. 28–9.

28 Text in Sasada Shigeru, *Nihon Shakaitō*, vol. 1, pp. 253–4.

29 *Asahi*, 12 December 1953.

30 See 'Seinenbu katsudō hōshin no mondaiten' (mimeo, Nihon Shakaitō, [probably December 1953]), and Nihon Shakaitō Tōkyō To Rengōkai Bunkyō Shibu Seinenbu, *et al.*, 'Yamaguchi mondai ni kansuru seimei' (mimeo, January 1954).

31 See, e.g., *Jiji*, 10 January 1953.

6 NEUTRALISM AND 'DEMOCRATIC SOCIALISM'

1 Text in *Jōhō Tsūshin*, 1 July 1952, pp. 1–5.

2 See Nihon Shakaitō Hombu, *Dokuritsu Nihon no dōhyō* (August 1952), pp. 6–7; *Jōhō Tsūshin*, 15 July 1952, pp. 3–16.

3 See, e.g., ibid., 1 January 1952, pp. 4–6 and 1 July 1952, pp. 1–5; *Kokkai Nippō*, 8 February 1951.

4 See Preparatory Committee, ASC, *Report of Preliminary Meeting for Asian*

Socialist Conference (Rangoon, March 1952), pp. 83–6, 99–100; ASC, Reports of Sub-Committees 'A', 'B' and 'C', Asian Socialist Conference (Rangoon, January 1953).
5 Text in Jōhō Tsūshin, 15 January 1953, pp. 3–22.
6 For definitive statements of these attitudes, see the party's Action Policy for 1952, in Nihon Rōdō Nenkan, 1954, pp. 670–2; Action Policy for 1953, in Jōhō Tsūshin, 15 January 1953, pp. 3–22.
7 Action Policy for 1952, Nihon Rōdō Nenkan, 1954, p. 671.
8 Action Policy for 1953, Jōhō Tsūshin, 15 January 1953, p. 15.
9 Action Policy for 1952, Nihon Rōdō Nenkan, 1954, p. 671. The Japanese government signed a bilateral peace treaty with Nationalist China in April 1952.
10 Action Policy for 1953, Jōhō Tsūshin, 15 January 1953, p. 12.
11 Ibid.
12 Ibid.
13 A version of the Minsharen declaration is given in Yomiuri, 9 March 1952.
14 See Asahi, 19 and 21 January 1952; Nihon Keizai, 23 March 1952; also Sasada Shigeru, Nihon Shakaitō, vol. 1, pp. 204–5.
15 Summarized in Yomiuri, 21 October 1953. For a Left Socialist criticism, see Shakai Taimusu, 27 October 1953. For accounts of the subsequent controversy in the party Policy Committee, see Yomiuri, 26, 27 and 28 November 1953. A closely related document seen by the writer did not enunciate the first of Sone's proposals (rearmament), but incorporated versions of the other two: Nihon Shakaitō Seisaku Shingikai, 'Gaikō hōshin' (mimeo, 26 November 1953).
16 Yomiuri, 26 November 1953.
17 Ibid., 1 December 1953.
18 Ibid.
19 Ibid., 28 November 1953.
20 Mainichi, 17 December 1953. The faction's general point of view was expressed in a pamphlet issued a few months earlier: Oka Ryōichi, 'Tōitsu no suishin ni kansuru teigen' (mimeo, Shakaishugi Seisaku Kenkyūkai, July 1953).
21 Asahi (evening edn), 10 January 1954.
22 Quoted in Nihon Rōdō Nenkan, 1956, pp. 739–41.
23 Ibid.

7   REUNIFICATION

1 Yomiuri, 24 July 1953.
2 Oka Ryōichi, 'Tōitsu no suishin ni kansuru teigen' (mimeo, Shakaishugi Seisaku Kenkyūkai, July 1953).
3 See, e.g., Asanuma Inejirō, 'Tōitsu undō no shutaisei to kakuho', Jōhō Tsūshin, 15 August 1953, p. 1.
4 Shakai Taimusu, 23 September 1953.
5 'Tōitsu mondai chōsa kenkyū iinkai' (mimeo, Nihon Shakaitō, 27 November 1953), p. 5.
6 See Mainichi, 1 July 1954.
7 Ibid., 2 July 1954.
8 Asahi, 20 May 1954.
9 This controversy is treated in some detail in Nihon Rōdō Nenkan, 1956, pp. 749–50.
10 Jiji, 24 October 1954.
11 Ibid., 4 February 1954; Yomiuri (evening edn), 26 June 1954.
12 Okada Sōji (Suzuki faction), interviewed 18 October 1962, said, however, that the Wada faction felt that unification could be obtained on better

terms if further postponed, because of LSP election successes, and that it
was only this issue that separated the Wada and Suzuki factions.
13 *Mainichi*, 2 July 1954.
14 Ibid., 6 August 1954.
15 Okada Sōji in October 1962 said that his firm statement of policy at this
stage was aimed principally at the Nishio faction, which was proving
intransigent.
16 See, e.g., Sone Eki, in Nihon Shakaitō Hombu, *Nihon no kanzen dokuritsu
to MSA enjo* (July 1953), pp. 20–1.
17 'Chūgoku shisetsudan hōkokusho', *Jōhō Tsūshin*, 1 November 1954,
pp. 3–12.
18 Previous RSP policy on Taiwan was that the island should be put provision-
ally under UN control; the UN should ensure that Taiwan did not become
a strategic threat to either camp and the ownership of the island should
be determined by the free will of the people of Taiwan. See for instance
Nihon Shakaitō Seisaku Shingikai, 'Gaikō hōshin' (mimeo, 26 November
1953), p. 3. The LSP policy on Taiwan was that the fate of the island
should be decided by the people of the whole of China, including Taiwan.
See LSP statement in Nihon Shakaitō Hombu, 'Shakaishugi Intanashonaru
dai 3 kai taikai, Ajia Shakaitō Kaigi dai 2 kai kanjikai, hōkokusho'
(mimeo, October 1953), p. 19.
19 *Jōhō Tsūshin*, 1 November 1954, pp. 3–12.
20 *Jiji*, 1 November 1954.
21 For an account of the differences between the two sides at this time, see
Asahi, 21 November 1954. The full text of the joint election platform is
given in *Nihon Rōdō Nenkan*, 1956, p. 761.
22 *Nihon Rōdō Nenkan*, 1956, p. 761.
23 LSP representation increased from seventy-two to eighty-nine seats. RSP
representation increased from sixty-six to sixty-seven seats.
24 *Asahi*, 9 March 1955.
25 Text in *Jōhō Tsūshin*, 15 May 1955, pp. 1–6.
26 *Asahi*, 18 May 1955.
27 Sasaki Kōzō, 'Suzuki iinchō no tōitsu ni kansuru Niigata danwa no
jitsujō', *Tō Katsudō*, 25 May 1955, p. 1.
28 *Mainichi*, 21 June 1955.
29 Ibid., 24 June 1955.
30 Katsumata Seiichi, reported in *Asahi*, 28 June 1955.
31 Ibid.
32 Text in Nihon Shakaitō Hombu, *Yakushin suru Nihon Shakaitō* (October
1955), pp. 47–72.
33 Ibid., p. 70.
34 *Asahi*, 20 September 1955.
35 *Yakushin suru Nihon Shakaitō*, pp. 70–2.
36 *Asahi*, 21 September 1955.
37 Ibid.
38 For details, see Yamazaki Hiroshi, *Nihon Shakaitō no jūnen shi*,
pp. 202–3.
39 See, e.g., Yanada Kōki, *Nihon Shakaitō* (Hōbunsha, 1956), pp. 1–22.

8 SUZUKI, ASANUMA AND 'POSITIVE NEUTRALITY'

1 It is difficult to agree with one writer that in foreign policy 'the victory
was substantially with the Right': D.C.S. Sissons. 'Recent Developments in
Japan's Socialist Movement' (1), *Far Eastern Survey*, March 1960, p. 43.
The Right had moved further from its 1951 position than had the Left,
and in the united platform the Left remained free to interpret 'self-

reliant independence' in the sense of non-alignment, abolition of the Security Treaty and a multilateral guarantee of a neutralist Japan.

2 See 'Futatabi kyakkō wo abiru chūritsu gaikō', *Shakai Taimusu*, 22 January 1958.

3 See, e.g., Sone Eki, 'Jishu dokuritsu no tachiba', *Nihon Shakai Shimbun*, 27 February 1956.

4 Action Policy for 1957, in *Shakai Shimpō*, 15 January 1957.

5 Ibid.

6 See D. C. Hellmann, 'Japanese Foreign Policy and Domestic Politics: The Peace Agreement with the Soviet Union' (unpubl. Ph.D. thesis, University of California, Berkeley, 1964); also *Yomiuri*, 26 August 1956.

7 Nihon Shakaitō Tōitsu Jumbi Iinkai, *Nihon Shakaitō kōryō, undō hōshin, seisaku taikō* (October 1955), pp. 85–6.

8 The positions of the two sides on this issue are compared in Nihon Shakaitō Tōitsu Jumbi Iinkai, *Tōitsu e no ayumi*, p. 95.

9 Quoted in Morishima Morito, 'Chūka Jimmin Kyōwakoku to no kokkō juritsu ni tsuite', *Shakai Tsūshin*, 1 July 1956.

10 Action Policy for 1957, in *Shakai Shimpō*, 15 January 1957.

11 Text in *Shakai Tsūshin*, 5 April 1957, pp. 1–2.

12 Text in *Nitchū no kokkō kaifuku e*, (Nihon Shakaitō, [probably April 1957]), pp. 143–6.

13 *Asahi*, 26 July 1957.

14 See, e.g., 'Sata hōkokusho', *Gekkan Shakaitō*, October 1958, pp. 18–19.

15 See, e.g., Nihon Shakaitō Hombu, 'Shōwa 33 nendo dai 2 kai chūō iinkai tōmu hōkokusho' (mimeo, January 1959), pp. 27–30.

16 *Asahi*, 20 November 1958. For a Japanese Socialist reaction, see Matsumoto Shichirō, 'Chin Ki seimei no igi', *Shakai Taimusu*, 27 November 1958.

17 *Seisaku to hōshin—Dai 16 kai teiki zenkoku taikai (1959–9) kettei* (Nihon Shakaitō, September 1959), pp. 173–81 (hereafter called *Seisaku to hōshin*). See also *Asahi*, 13 and 30 January 1959.

18 See 'Futatabi kyakkō wo abiru chūritsu gaikō', *Shakai Taimusu*, 22 January 1958.

19 *Seisaku to hōshin*, p. 177.

20 See Yamaguchi Fusao, *Chūritsu, kono minzoku no kadai*, pp. 185–96.

21 See, e.g., Nihon Shakaitō Seisaku Shingikai, 'Hikakubusō sengen', *Seishin Shiryō*, 15 May 1958, p. 42.

22 'Futatabi kyakkō wo abiru chūritsu gaikō', *Shakai Taimusu*, 22 January 1958. See also Yamaguchi Fusao, 'Chūritsu chitai no settei e', *Gekkan Shakaitō*, February 1959, pp. 58–63.

23 See, e.g., Akamatsu Isamu, 'Nihon Kyōsantō no "chūritsu seisaku"', *Gekkan Shakaitō*, March 1959, pp. 48–50.

24 See Kamiyama Shigeo, 'Chūritsu wa dokuritsu no michi de aru', *Zenei*, February 1959, pp. 9–17.

25 See, e.g., editorial comment in *Asahi*, 24 March 1959.

26 Chiba Makoto, 'Chūgoku to Shakaitō no tachiba', *Hokkaidō Shimbun* (evening edn), 17 January 1962.

27 Okada Sōji, interviewed 18 October 1962.

28 Part of this account corresponds with a report in *Asahi*, 28 March 1959. Other Socialists interviewed attributed Asanuma's statement to lack of sophistication in the finer points of doctrine, emotional reaction to situations and susceptibility to manipulation.

29 In this section a debt must be acknowledged to the following article (published in two parts): D. C. S. Sissons, 'Recent Developments in Japan's Socialist Movement', *Far Eastern Survey*, March 1960, pp. 40–7, and June 1960, pp. 89–92.

30 The JSP gained only six seats and a 2.7 per cent increase in its total vote over the combined socialist total in 1955. The 1958 party Congress also

Notes (Chapters 8–9)   181

showed disquiet over failure to expand its organization and membership. See Sissons, 'Recent Developments in Japan's Socialist Movement' (1), pp. 44–5.

31 Sakisaka Itsurō, 'Tadashii kōryō, tadashii kikō', Shakaishugi, December 1958, pp. 46–52.

32 The matter is discussed in Taguchi Fukuji, Nihon no kakushin seiryoku, pp. 171–3.

33 Asahi, 25 December 1958.

34 See especially Nishio Suehiro, 'Tō no shutaisei kakuritsu wa shikkōbu kara', Gekkan Shakaitō, September 1958, pp. 11–15.

35 See Sone Eki, 'Tō no saiken ni atatte no jakkan no mondaiten', Gekkan Shakaitō, August 1959, pp. 38–42; Sone Eki and Okada Haruo, 'Chūritsu mondai wo megutte', Gekkan Shakaitō, March 1959, pp. 39–47.

36 At the JSP Congress held in March 1960, Asanuma was challenged for the Chairmanship (after the retirement of Suzuki) by his factional colleague Kawakami.

9 'POSITIVE NEUTRALITY' AND 'STRUCTURAL REFORM'

1 See R. A. Scalapino and J. Masumi, Parties and Politics in Contemporary Japan; G. R. Packard, Protest in Tokyo: the Security Treaty Crisis of 1960.

2 See Nihon Shakai Shimbun, 4 July 1960; Shakai Shimpō, 31 July 1960.

3 'Waga tō no "seiji hōshin kaisetsu" ni taisuru Kyōsantō no hihan ni kotaeru', Shakai Shimpō, 14 August 1960.

4 'Chūritsuron e no hihan ni kotaeru', ibid., 28 August 1960.

5 'Nihon Shakaitō wa u-keika shita ka. Nihon Kyōsantō no hihan ni kotaeru', ibid., 18 December 1960.

6 See Asahi, 15 July 1961.

7 Text in Gekkan Shakaitō, March 1962, pp. 99–101.

8 Chiba Makoto, 'Chūgoku to Shakaitō no tachiba', Hokkaidō Shimbun (evening edn), 17 January 1962.

9 Suzuki Mosaburō, 'Dai 3-ji hō-Chū shisetsudan no seika', Gekkan Shakaitō, March 1962, pp. 95–8.

10 Asahi (evening edn), 3 August 1962.

11 Abridged text in Kokumin Seiji Nenkan, 1962, p. 136.

12 Ibid., pp. 136–7.

13 Shakai Shimpō, 13 August 1961.

14 Akahata, 1 and 8 September 1961.

15 Eda Saburō, 'Kaku jikken akumade hantai', Shakai Shimpō, 24 September 1961.

16 Opinion expressed by Hososako Kanemitsu, interviewed 22 February 1963 together with three other members of Heiwa Dōshikai.

17 Text in Kokumin Seiji Nenkan, 1962, pp. 138–9.

18 See ibid., 1963, pp. 166–8; Akahata, 7, 8 and 9 August 1962; Shakai Shimpō, 19 August 1962.

19 See Asahi, 6 and 7 August 1963.

20 See, e.g., Shakai Shimpō, 1 January 1962.

21 See, e.g., Sakisaka Itsurō, 'Tadashii kōryō, tadashii kikō', Shakaishugi, December 1958, pp. 46–52.

22 The stagnation in the party's electoral fortunes first revealed at the Lower House election of May 1958 was still evident in the Lower House election of November 1960. In 1958 the Socialist percentage of total votes was 32.94. In 1960 it had dropped to 27.56. If we add, however, the 8.77 per cent obtained by the newly formed DSP, we see that the total socialist vote had risen to 37.33 per cent.

23 Asahi (evening edn), 25 March 1963.

24 See ibid., 22 November 1961.

25 See, e.g., Katsumata Seiichi, quoted in *Yomiuri*, 11 January 1961.
26 M.P.s could, however, still become delegates with the consent of the Central Executive Committee, and in any case had the right to attend and speak at the congress.
27 See *Nihon Keizai*, 21 March 1961; *Asahi*, 19 December 1961.
28 See *Mainichi*, 27 December 1960.
29 See *Asahi*, 17 December 1961.
30 Satō Noboru, 'Shakaishugi to Chūritsu', *Shisō*, October 1961, pp. 34–43.
31 For instance, in *Shakai Shimpō*, 19 November 1961.
32 See Wada Hiroo, 'Chūritsu seisaku no zenshin no tame ni', *Chūō Kōron*, June 1962, pp. 98–106; Wada Hiroo, 'Sekkyoku chūritsu to daisan seiryoku', *Gekkan Shakaitō*, November 1962, pp. 63–8.
33 Wada Hiroo, 'Sekkyoku chūritsu to daisan seiryoku', *Gekkan Shakaitō*, November 1962, pp. 63–4.
34 For text and amendments, see *Gekkan Shakaitō*, December 1961, pp. 4–28.
35 See especially *Asahi*, 11 December 1961.

10   NEUTRALIST ECLIPSE?

1 Quoted in Wada Takayoshi, 'Shakaitō no riron to kōdō no rakusa', *Asahi Janaru*, 18 December 1966.
2 See, e.g., Matsumoto's arguments in Matsumoto Shichirō and Ishibashi Masashi, 'Nanajūnen e no Shakaitō no shinro', *Gendai no Me*, December 1966, pp. 88–91.
3 For a collection of the principal documents and articles in the 'vision' controversy, see Nakajima Iwao (ed.), *Shakaishugi no bijiyon ronsō* (Shinano shoten, 1962).
4 In *Shakai Taimusu*, 22 January 1953.
5 See *Asahi*, 28 and 30 November 1962.
6 See *Sekai*, July 1965, pp. 156–9.
7 Matsumoto Shichirō and Ishibashi Masashi, op. cit.
8 Quoted in *Asahi*, 27 August 1966.
9 Ibid., 7 May 1965. For amplification of his views, see Sasaki Kōzō, 'Sensō soshi to San-In-sen shori e zenryoku wo kesshū shiyō', *Gekkan Shakaitō*, July 1965, pp. 2–5.
10 *Ekonomisuto*, 8 February 1966, pp. 36–9. See also *Yomiuri*, 10 January 1966.
11 According to a source who may not be identified.
12 *Yomiuri*, 20 January 1966.
13 For an analysis of recent trends in the JCP, see J.A.A. Stockwin, 'The Communist Party of Japan', *Problems of Communism*, vol. 16, no. 1, 1967, pp. 1–10.
14 *Asahi*, 4 December 1966.
15 *Tōkyō*, 1 January 1967 (as translated in American Embassy, Tokyo, *Daily Summary of Japanese Press*, 6 January 1967).
16 See, e.g., *Asahi*, 18 August 1965.
17 *Nihon Keizai*, 13 July 1964.
18 Ibid., 18 October 1964.
19 For the text of the communiqué, and commentaries, see ibid., 30 October 1964.
20 The views expressed in this paragraph and the next are derived from information supplied by sources who may not be identified.
21 See *Ekonomisuto*, 8 February 1966, pp. 36–9.
22 *Shakai Shimpō*, 26 January 1966.
23 In September 1965, for instance, Katsumata, the then Foreign Policy Bureau Chairman, led a delegation to Indonesia, the United Arab Republic and Algeria, and also managed to assuage the fears of the Socialist Interna-

tional that the JSP was joining the 'Chinese' camp. See *Asahi*, 17 September and 5 October 1965.

24 *Asahi*, 10 December 1966.

25 See, e.g., J. A. A. Stockwin, 'Japanese Attitudes to the Sino-Soviet Dispute', *International Journal*, vol. 18, no. 4, 1963, pp. 488–500.

26 See, e.g., speech quoted in *Asahi*, 22 May 1965.

27 See Ishibashi Masashi, 'Hibusō, chūritsu e no michi', *Gekkan Shakaitō*, July 1966, pp. 49–52.

II ASPECTS OF THE NEUTRALIST BLUEPRINT

1 See Ishibashi Masashi, 'Hibusō, chūritsu e no michi', *Gekkan Shakaitō*, July 1966, pp. 49–52.

2 Sakisaka Itsurō, 'Nihon no saigumbi wo meguru shomondai', *Jōhō Tsūshin*, 15 March 1951, pp. 11–22.

3 See, e.g., Tanaka Shinjirō, 'Nihon wa ikani shite sensō no kengai ni tachiuru ka—Nihon no chūritsuron ni kanshite', *Sekai Hyōron*, June 1949, pp. 1–13.

4 See, e.g., Yamaguchi Fusao, *Chūritsu, kono minzoku no kadai*, p. 202.

5 See, e.g., Yokota Kisaburō, 'Nihon no kokusai shōrai', *Shakaishugi*, November 1946, pp. 33–9. This writer later came strongly to reject neutrality.

6 'We, the Japanese people, desire peace for all time and are deeply conscious of the highest ideals controlling human relationships, and we have determined to preserve our security and existence, *trusting in the justice and faith of the peace-loving peoples of world*.' (my italics).

7 See, e.g., Nihon Shakaitō Hombu, *Yakushin suru Nihon Shakaitō* (1955), pp. 70–1.

8 Sakamoto Yoshikazu, 'Chūritsu Nihon no bōei kōsō: Nichi-Bei ampo taisei ni kawaru mono', *Sekai*, August 1959, pp. 31–47.

9 See, e.g., *Sekai*, September 1959, pp. 231–3.

10 See speech by Hanyū Sanshichi, in *Kampō (gōgai)*, 27 April 1950, pp. 901–2.

11 See, e.g., Ryū Shintarō, 'Chūritsu taisei e no michi: rengō shokoku ni uttau', *Bungei Shunjū*, January 1950, pp. 22–7.

12 See, e.g., Yamakawa Hitoshi, 'Hibusō chūritsu wa fukanō ka', *Sekai*, July 1952, pp. 22–34.

13 Yamaguchi, op. cit., p. 211.

14 See, e.g., Ishibashi Masashi, op. cit.

15 Yokota Kisaburō, 'Eisei chūritsuron wo hihan suru', *Zenshin*, July 1949, pp. 28–36. See also 'Zasshi tembō', in *Yomiuri*, 29 June 1949.

16 See Mutō Unjūrō, 'Zemmen kōwa no hōritsuteki kiso', *Jōhō Tsūshin*, 1 July 1950, pp. 6–23.

17 Ryū Shintarō, op. cit.

18 Heiwa Mondai Danwakai, 'Mitabi heiwa ni tsuite, Heiwa Mondai Danwakai kenkyū hōkoku', *Sekai*, December 1950, pp. 21–52.

19 The reasons for this were explored in a number of articles by another nonsocialist international lawyer, Taoka Ryōichi, who in 1949–51 engaged Yokota in extended debate on the issue of neutrality. See Taoka Ryōichi, 'Eisei chūritsuron no tachiba kara', *Zenshin*, September 1949, pp. 38–47.

20 See, e.g., *Jōhō Tsūshin*, 1 July 1950, pp. 1–3.

21 See the remarks of the then Foreign Minister Shiina Etsusaburō, quoted in *Yomiuri*, 25 April 1966.

22 See Ishibashi Masashi, op. cit.

23 Ibid.

24 See for instance the remarks of Katsumata Seiichi, in *Shakai Taimusu*, 1 March 1953.

25 Yamaguchi Fusao, interviewed 13 June 1962. See also Yamaguchi Fusao, 'Hibusō chūritsu no genjitsusei: eisei chūritsu e no michi', *Jiyū*, July 1961, pp. 62–8.

26 See Sugiyama Shōzō, 'Betonamu heiwa e no mosaku; minoranu kakkoku no heiwa teian', *Gekkan Shakaitō*, January 1967, pp. 51–8.
27 Frank Langdon, *Politics in Japan*, p. 279.
28 See Yamaguchi Fusao, 'Chūritsu, gunshuku to kaku senryaku no kanren; Betonamu sensō no hitotsu no sokumen kara', *Gekkan Shakaitō*, January 1967, pp. 43–50.

12 THE JSP: A SOCIALIST PARTY WITH A DIFFERENCE

1 See, e.g., D. Healey, *A Neutral Belt in Europe* (London, 1958), especially p. 15.
2 The difference in the relative electoral strength of Communists and Socialists in Italy and Japan may be seen from the following table:

Election year	% of total vote			
	Italy		Japan	
	PCI	PSI	JCP	JSP
1953	22.6	12.8	1.9	26.6*
1958	22.7	14.2	2.6	32.9

*LSP and RSP combined.

3 I.e. those who wanted 'fusion' with the PCI.
4 Quoted in G. Galli, *La Sinistra Italiana nel Dopoguerra* (Bologna, 1958), p. 177.
5 Ibid.
6 See R. Zariski, 'The Italian Socialist Party: A Case Study in Factional Conflict', *American Political Science Review*, vol. 56, no. 2, 1962, pp. 372–90; also A. Landolfi, 'Partito Socialista Italiano: Struttura, organi dirigenti, correnti', *Tempi Moderni*, January-March 1962, pp. 3–45.
7 See S. Neumann (ed.), *Modern Political Parties* (Chicago, 1956), pp. 395–421.
8 Landolfi, op. cit., p. 13.
9 Ibid, p. 12.
10 Ibid., pp. 22–3.
11 Taguchi Fukuji, *Nihon no kakushin seiryoku*, p. 18.
12 M. Duverger, *Political Parties; their Organisation and Activity in the Modern State* (London, 1954), pp. 17–23.
13 See table of election results, chapter 1, n. 1.
14 Figures from *Asahi*, 30 November 1966.
15 See J. Kyōgoku and N. Ike, 'Urban-Rural Differences in Voting Behaviour in Postwar Japan', *Economic Development and Cultural Change*, vol. 9, no. 1, part 2, 1960, pp. 167–85.
16 Figures from *Nihon Keizai*, 31 December 1966.
17 See Andō Nihei, 'Nihon-gata shakai minshushugi tō no yukikata', *Gendai no Me*, December 1966, pp. 56–65; also *Mainichi*, 28 November 1966.

BIBLIOGRAPHY

JAPANESE-LANGUAGE SOURCES

Of the Japanese-language sources used in the preparation of this book only the most important are listed here; others may be found in the notes. For further source material on Japanese left wing movements in general, readers are referred to the meticulously compiled bibliography by Uyehara, listed on page 188. An extensive selection of books and articles on neutrality and neutralism published up to 1960 in Japanese (and other languages including English) is to be found in *Chūritsushugi no kenkyū*, vol. 2, pp. 461-506.

Books, Articles and Party Materials

Akamatsu Katsumaro, *Nihon shakai undō shi (History of the Japanese Socialist Movement)*. Iwanami Shinsho, 1952.

Chūritsushugi no kenkyū (Studies of Neutralism). 2 vols. Nihon Kokusai Mondai Kenkyūjo, 1961.

Heiwa Mondai Danwakai, 'Mitabi heiwa ni tsuite, Heiwa Mondai Danwakai kenkyū hōkoku' ('Third Statement on Peace: Study Report of the Discussion Circle on Problems of Peace'), *Sekai*, December 1950.

Ishibashi Masashi, 'Hibusō, chūritsu e no michi' ('The Road to Disarmament and Neutralism'), *Gekkan Shakaitō*, July 1966.

Kōno Mitsu, *Nihon shakai seitō shi (History of Japanese Socialist Political Parties)*. Chūō Kōronsha, 1960.

Maeshiba Kakuzō and Yamate Haruyuki (eds), *Chūritsu wa jitsugen dekiru ka (Can Neutralism be Achieved?)*. Sanichi Shobō, 1961.

Nihon Shakaitō Tōitsu Jumbi Iinkai, *Tōitsu e no ayumi (The Road to Unification)*. Nihon Shakaitō (LSP), [? October 1955].

Okakura Koshirō, *Dai san seiryoku, chūritsu to heiwa (Third Force, Neutralism and Peace)*. Kaname Shobō, 1953.

Sakamoto Yoshikazu, 'Chūritsu Nihon no bōei kōsō: Nichi-Bei ampo taisei ni kawaru mono', *Sekai*, August 1959.

Sakisaka Itsurō, 'Nihon no saigumbi ni kansuru shomondai' ('Some Questions Concerning the Rearmamant of Japan'), *Jōhō Tsūshin*, 15 March 1951.

Sasada Shigeru, *Nihon Shakaitō (The Japan Socialist Party)*. 2 vols. Sanichi Shobō, 1960.

Satō Noboru, 'Shakaishugi to chūritsu' ('Socialism and Neutralism'), *Shisō*, October 1961.

Taguchi Fukuji, *Nihon no kakushin seiryoku (Japan's Progressive Forces)*. Kōbundō, 1961.

Taoka Ryōichi, 'Eisei chūritsuron no tachiba kara' ('From the Standpoint of Permanent Neutrality'), *Zenshin*, September 1949.

Wada Hiroo, 'Chūritsu seisaku no zenshin no tame ni' ('For the Advancement of a Neutralist Policy'), *Chūō Kōron*, June 1962.

Yakushin suru Nihon Shakaitō (The Advancing Japan Socialist Party). Nihon Shakaitō (RSP), October 1955.

Yamaguchi Fusao, *Chūritsu, kono minzoku no kadai (Neutralism, a Question for this Nation)*. Shiseidō, 1959.

Yamazaki Hiroshi, *Nihon Shakaitō no jūnen shi (Ten Year History of the Japan Socialist Party)*. Taibunkan, 1956.

Yanada Kōki, *Nihon Shakaitō (The Japan Socialist Party)*. Hōbunsha, 1956.

Yokota Kisaburō, 'Eisei chūritsuron no tachiba kara' ('Criticizing the Permanent Neutrality Argument'), *Zenshin*, July 1949.

Newspapers and Periodicals

Japan Socialist Party

Gekkan Shakaitō (Monthly Socialist Party); JSP, 1957–

Jōhō Tsūshin (News Bulletin): JSP, 1950–1; RSP, 1951–5; succeeded by *Shakai Tsūshin*

Kokumin Seiji Nenkan (People's Political Year Book); JSP, 1962–

Nihon Shakai Shimbun (Japan Socialist Newspaper): RSP, 1951–5; JSP (right wing factions), 1955–60

Shakai Shimbun (Socialist Newspaper): JSP, 1945–51; succeeded by *Nihon Shakai Shimbun*.

Shakai Shimpō (Socialist News): JSP (close to Suzuki faction), 1955–60; controlled by Structural Reform faction, 1960–5

Shakai Taimusu (Socialist Times); Shakai Taimusu Sha, 1952–5 (supporting LSP), and 1956–60 (close to Wada faction of JSP)

Shakai Tsūshin (Socialist Bulletin); JSP 1955–?
Shakaishugi (Socialism); Shakaishugi Kyōkai, 1950– (supporting
   left wing socialist factions)
Tō Katsudō (Party Activities): LSP, 1951–5; succeeded by
   Shakai Shimpō
Zenshin (Progress): Itagaki Shoten, 1947–50 (supporting left
   wing socialist factions); succeeded by *Shakaishugi*
General

Asahi Nenkan	*Nihon Keizai Shimbun*
Asahi Shimbun	*Nihon Rōdō Nenkan*
Chūō Kōron	*Sekai*
Jiyū	*Sōhyō*
Kampō (gōgai)	*Yomiuri Shimbun*
Mainichi Shimbun	*Zenei*

ENGLISH-LANGUAGE SOURCES

Bonjour, E., *Swiss Neutrality, its History and Meaning*. London,
   1946.
Cohn, G., *Neo-Neutrality*. New York, 1939.
Colbert, E. S., *The Left Wing in Japanese Politics*. New York,
   1952.
Cole, A. B., Totten, G. O. and Uyehara, C. H., *Socialist Parties
   in Postwar Japan*. New Haven, 1966.
Healey, D., *Neutralism*. London, 1955.
Ike, N., *Japanese Politics: An Introductory Survey*. New York,
   1957.
Kawai, K., *Japan's American Interlude*. Chicago, 1960.
Jessup, P. C., *Neutrality, its History, Economics and Law*.
   4 vols. New York, 1936.
Journal of Social and Political Ideas in Japan, vol. 3, no. 1,
   1965. (Whole issue devoted to the left wing movement in
   Japan.)
Langdon, F., *Politics in Japan*. Boston, 1967.
Levine, S. B., *Industrial Relations in Postwar Japan*. Urbana,
   1958.
Lyon, P., *Neutralism*. Leicester, 1963.
Maruyama, M., *Thought and Behaviour in Modern Japanese
   Politics*. London, 1963.
Mendel, D. H., *The Japanese People and Foreign Policy: A
   Study of Public Opinion in Post-Treaty Japan*. Berkeley, 1961.
Miller, J. D. B., *The Politics of the Third World*. London, 1966.

Morgenthau, H., 'Neutrality and Neutralism', in *Dilemmas of Politics*. Chicago, 1958.
Morris, I. I., 'Japanese Foreign Policy and Neutralism', *International Affairs*. January 1960.
Packard, G. R., *Protest in Tokyo: The Security Treaty Crisis of 1960*. London, 1966.
Passin, H., 'The Sources of Protest in Japan', *American Political Science Review*, vol. 56, no. 2, 1962.
—— (ed.), *The United States and Japan*. Englewood Cliffs, 1966.
Scalapino, R. A., ' "Neutralism" in Asia', *American Political Science Review*, vol. 48, no. 1, 1954.
——, *Democracy and the Party Movement in Prewar Japan: The Failure of the First Attempt*. Berkeley, 1953.
——, *The Japanese Communist Movement 1920–1966*. Berkeley, 1967.
——, and Masumi, J., *Parties and Politics in Contemporary Japan*. Berkeley, 1962.
Sissons, D. C. S., 'Recent Developments in Japan's Socialist Movement', *Far Eastern Survey*, March and June 1960.
——, 'The Pacifist Clause of the Japanese Constitution', *International Affairs*, January 1961.
—— (ed.), *Papers on Modern Japan, 1965*. Canberra, 1965.
Stockwin, J. A. A., 'Japanese Attitudes to the Sino-Soviet Dispute', *International Journal*, vol. 18, no. 4, 1963.
——, 'The Japanese Socialist Party under New Leadership', *Asian Survey*, vol. 6, no. 4, 1966.
——, 'The Communist Party of Japan', *Problems of Communism*, vol. 16, no. 1, 1967.
Swearingen, R. and Langer, P. F., *Red Flag in Japan*. Cambridge, Mass., 1952.
Totten, G. O., *The Social Democratic Movement in Prewar Japan*. New Haven, 1966.
——, and Kawakami, T., 'The Functions of Factionalism in Japanese Politics', *Pacific Affairs*, vol. 38, no. 2, 1965.
Uyehara, C. H., *Leftwing Social Movements in Japan, an Annotated Bibliography*. Tokyo, 1959.
Ward, R. E., 'The Commission on the Constitution and the Prospects for Constitutional Change in Japan', *Journal of Asian Studies*, vol. 24, no. 3, 1965.
——, 'Political Modernization and Political Culture in Japan', *World Politics*, vol. 15, no. 4, 1963.
Zariski, R., 'The Italian Socialist Party: A Case Study in Fac-

tional Conflict', *American Political Science Review*, vol. 56, no. 2, 1962.

Unpublished source

Hellmann, D. C., 'Japanese Foreign Policy and Domestic Politics: The Peace Agreement with the Soviet Union', Ph.D. thesis, University of California, Berkeley, 1964.

INDEX

WAYNESBURG COLLEGE LIBRARY
WAYNESBURG, PA.

WAYNESBURG COLLEGE LIBRARY
WAYNESBURG, PA.

329.952   S866j
Stockwin, James Arthur Ainscow
The Japanese Socialist Party and Neutralism
84347